About the (GW00600750

Barry Divola's previous books are *Fanclub, Searching for Kingly Critter,* and *M Is For Metal* (with Paul McNeil). He won the Banjo Paterson Award for short fiction in 2004, 2005 and 2006 for the stories 'Nipple', 'Cicada Boy' and 'Nixon'. He is the music critic for *Who,* a columnist for *the (sydney) magazine,* a senior writer for *Rolling Stone,* and regularly contributes to *Sunday Life, Madison, Entertainment Weekly* and other magazines and newspapers. He is also a music and popular culture commentator on ABC 702 Radio. When not on the road, he lives in Sydney with a cat named Uma.

By the same author

Fanclub
Searching for Kingly Critter
M *is for Metal* (with Paul McNeil)

THE SECRET LIFE OF BACKPACKERS

A bunk's-eye view of the tourist trail from Bondi to Cairns

Barry Divola

ABC
Books

Published by ABC Books for the
AUSTRALIAN BROADCASTING CORPORATION
GPO BOX 9994 Sydney NSW 2001

Copyright © Barry Divola 2008

First published January 2008

All rights reserved. No part of this publication may be reproduced, sorted in a retrieval system, or transmitted, in any form or by any means, electronic, mechanical, photocopying, recording or otherwise, without the prior written permission of the Australian Broadcasting Corporation.

National Library of Australia
Cataloguing in Publication entry

Divola, Barry.
    The secret lives of backpackers : a bunk's-eye view of the tourist
    trail from Bondi to Cairns.

    ISBN 978 07333 2092 7 (pbk.).

    1. Divola, Barry – Travel. 2. Backpacking – Social aspects
    – New South Wales. 3. Backpacking – Social aspects –
    Queensland. 4. Independent travel – Social aspects – New
    South Wales. 5. Independent travel – Social aspects –
    Queensland. 6. New South Wales – Description and travel.
    7. Queensland – Description and travel. I. Australian
    Broadcasting Corporation. II. Title.

910.4

Cover design by Josh Durham, Design by Committee
Typeset in 11.5 on 18pt Sabon by Kirby Jones
Printed in Australia by Griffin Press, Adelaide

5 4 3 2 1

For my friend Twit,
who's always got my back.

'I love to go a-wandering,
Along the mountain track,
And as I go, I love to sing,
My knapsack on my back.'

– The Happy Wanderer

'Things change over long distance.'

– The Go-Betweens, 'Bye Bye Pride'

'Here began all our troubles.'

– Lieutenant James Cook, after his ship
Endeavour ran aground near Cape Tribulation.

Contents

Part 1   Bondi   1

Part 2   Byron Bay   89

Part 3   Hervey Bay and Fraser Island   151

Part 4   Airlie Beach and the Whitsundays   193

Part 5   Cairns   235

PART 1

BONDI

There were five people in the room, and four of them were having sex. I was the other guy.

It was four o'clock in the morning. It was my last night as a backpacker in Cairns, northern Queensland. I was not getting laid. But someone else obviously was.

I'd met my two female room-mates earlier in the evening. Kat and Rachel were 20-year-old best buddies from Manchester. Kat was birdlike, Rachel was chunky. They finished each other's sentences and laughed like drunk kookaburras. They were like the two sweet, ditzy girls who were incidental characters in every pub in every British sitcom of the 1970s. It was also their final night in Cairns, as they were heading south and making their way to Sydney to find work.

'We just met the other two guys in the room,' Rachel told me after introducing herself. 'They're Australian, like you.'

'They're coming back later with bottles of passionfruit champagne, which sounds nice,' Kat added.

Well, I thought, it would sound nice if you had never drunk anything in your life before apart from sugar-sweetened diesel fuel.

'They're getting a bottle for each of us!' exclaimed Rachel, as if this was a good thing. She didn't go up on tippy-toes and clap her hands together at this comment, but if she suddenly did, I wouldn't have been at all surprised.

It is a truth universally acknowledged that guys buying champagne for girls—even if it's el cheapo passion pop—must be in want of sex.

'So, I guess I'll see you later,' I said, after having a shower, dressing, and heading towards the door of our room in search of dinner. 'But should we have some sort of signal if you get lucky, like hanging a bra on the door handle or something?'

The kookaburras started up again. Rachel gave me a light punch on the arm.

'What are you like?' she squealed. 'It's not like that.'

Seven hours later it was, in fact, exactly like that. I'd got in after three a.m. They got in half an hour later. And they got into it 4 minutes after that.

Kat had trouble finding her bed, but when she did, she and her bloke started making the unmistakable mating call of the squeaky bedsprings. Rachel and her guy were at it on the bed opposite, the bedclothes undulating in a most unslumber-like manner. Then Kat and her guy started giggling. Perhaps they were getting self-conscious. They adjourned to the bathroom and turned on the shower. The muffled moans drifting through the door into my right ear provided a stereo accompaniment to the wet noises from the other couple in my left ear.

'I'll know when to stop,' Rachel's guy said, in a whisper that the people in the room next door could have heard.

'Nuh-uh,' she replied.

Someone had obviously spent all his money on passion pop and none on condoms.

'Yes I will.'

'No you won't.'

'Will.'

'Won't.'

'What'll we do then?'

And that's when she went down on him. For the next 20 minutes. I had to admire her stamina. And his. I couldn't do much else, as I was certainly not getting any sleep. Or anything else for that matter.

As I lay there in the semi-dark and the tropical heat, listening to the sound of people apart from myself having sex, my mind wandered.

What on earth was I doing? How on earth had I arrived here at this point? And why on earth had I done it so willingly? It's not as if I didn't know what I was getting myself into. The fact is that I was experiencing deja vu.

In January 2006, I had spent seven days and seven nights in a Bondi backpacker hostel to research and write a magazine article. And yes, if seven days and seven nights sounds vaguely biblical, as if it should be accompanied by plagues of locusts, seven-headed beasts, and lakes of fire and sulphur, then you're halfway there.

My introduction to that Bondi hostel was the drunk, stoned proprietor thrashing away at an acoustic guitar while people were trying to book in.

'You can check out any time you like, but you can never leave,' he had howled.

Never before had The Eagles sounded so prophetic, or so foreboding. That line would come back to haunt me because a year later I decided to do it all again. But not just for a week—this time for a month. And not just in Bondi. This time I would take to the road, following the well-trodden trail up the east coast of Australia, from Bondi to Cairns.

Before I go any further, I should point out here that even though my mother still refers to me as a young man, she is in the minority. Forty is in my rear-vision mirror. Hair is a distant memory. There are crevices on my face that can no longer be politely referred to as smile lines. Saturday nights are not all right for fighting, but perhaps just fine for lying on the couch.

My journey into the valley of the backpackers was going to be as much a battle with my own will, stamina and patience as it would be an expedition into the wild and exotic world of the budget traveller.

Before that week in Bondi in 2006, my trusty green backpack had been out of service for some time. It saw active duty in the United Kingdom, Europe and the Middle East in 1986/1987. It circumnavigated the United States in the belly of various Greyhound buses in 1991. But it was finally retired a decade ago for a sturdy case with wheels and a retractable handle—a case that once a year left Sydney barely half full of clothes, and returned bulging with books, CDs, magazines, trinkets and cool stuff from New York three or four weeks later. This was how I travelled now.

But I took the backpack out of storage, dusted off the cobwebs, removed a few old baggage tags, and just the act of looping those straps over my arms and feeling the heft of the thing across my shoulders made me think about being in my twenties.

I used to be intrepid when I had this on my back. I've got the travel diaries to prove it. I hitch-hiked around England, Wales, Ireland, and Scotland. I did the same in Turkey, even though I'd seen *Midnight Express*. I trusted long-haul truck drivers. I trusted carpet shop salesmen. I trusted families who crammed me into the back of their tiny cars with their dogs and shopping. I trusted a guy in Northern Ireland who picked me up in his sports car and throughout the course of conversation said that he couldn't really tell me what he did for a living, but he showed me his gun and said, 'Let's just say I carry this around as part of my work.' And I trusted the UK travel agent who told me I could get a tourist visa at the border of every country I was travelling through from Vienna to Istanbul.

It turns out I should not have trusted this person as I was taken off a train at the border of Yugoslavia and Bulgaria, had my passport confiscated, was marched through the snow at two o'clock in the morning, and locked into a room with eight other bewildered travellers until daylight, when we were put onto another train that took us back the way we had come.

I chose countries on a whim. I lived my life day to day. I made vague plans and then changed them. Israel didn't seem that far from Turkey. Why not? And look, Egypt is just down there. Let's go. I wrote rambling letters and bad poetry. I became infatuated with girls of different nations and followed a couple of them across time zones to their home countries.

But that was twenty years ago. I look back and think about those times and get happily exhausted just reliving the memories. Surely there existed some in the backpacker population of 2007 who craved adventure and romance, who welcomed the exhilaration of venturing outside their safety zone, of creating their world each morning depending on where they decided to go or who they decided to talk to. I'm sure I'd experience the partying, the boredom, the drunkenness, the annoyances, the flirtation and the horror on this trip. But if I went further and longer and deeper into their world, would some faint echoes from my past travels emerge? Or would things just get uglier?

Why were the backpackers here? Where did they go? What did they talk about? What did they get up to? What did they think? What did they drink? What did they complain about? What did they think of Australia and Australians? What did they think of each other? What goes on at three o'clock in the morning? Did national stereotypes hold up? And how do you smoke drugs using an apple and a cigarette lighter?

To answer these questions I needed a dorm's-eye view. I needed to hang out in tourist pubs, dance to the Scissor Sisters with 19-year-old Swiss girls, and spend days living and travelling with these people in bars and buses and boats and beaches and bunks.

People can forget a lot of things in 12 months. I obviously had. For that one week a year ago, I was not so much an embedded journalist as I was an embunked journalist. I came out of it a babbling, sleep-deprived fool with my sanity and my liver barely intact.

I should have heeded the wise words uttered by a philosopher I met on the last night of my first backpacker stint in Bondi. Well, he wasn't exactly a philosopher. He was just a drunk Irish guy. But in an indication of how deep I'd gone into this thing, he was making perfect sense to me, and seemed incapable of slurring anything less than total wisdom for the hour he bent my ear.

'There are three types of people that stay here, Barry,' he told me, curling an arm around my shoulders and taking a slug of his tenth beer, then pointing his bottle towards the hostel stairs going up to the rooms. 'Some walk up the stairs two at a time. They're only staying here three days. Some walk up the stairs one at a time. They're staying two weeks.'

He paused dramatically, and valiantly tried to focus his eyes in a look that I presumed was meant to make me say something.

'And who are the third group of people?' I asked.

'They never walk up the stairs,' he said. 'They're here forever.'

The next morning I took the stairs three at a time to get out of there.

Exactly 12 months later, I shouldered my backpack, closed my front door behind me, and, wondering what adventures awaited me, I squinted wistfully into the middle distance.

That's when I realised I'd left my sunglasses behind, so I swore under my breath, unlocked the door, went back in again, found them, and then I was on my way.

As Albert Einstein, a man nearly as wise as a drunk Irish backpacker, once said, the definition of insanity is doing the same thing over and over again and expecting different results. He also said that the monotony and solitude of a quiet life stimulates the creative mind. Albert obviously didn't spend much of his time backpacking. He was on his way to formulating the theory of relativity, winning the Nobel Prize in Physics, and being named the most important person of the twentieth century by *Time* magazine. I was on my way to the 380 bus.

I encountered my first whingeing Pom in the first 10 minutes of my journey, and I was nowhere near Bondi yet.

At the time I was living in Manly, a Sydney seaside suburb which is trying desperately to be Bondi, but is fortunately failing, which is why I kind of like it. Despite a couple of cosmopolitan bars and a strip of upmarket restaurants, it's still a bit daggy, a bit faded, a bit old school. No matter how hard Manly tried it would always be Bondi's less attractive, less glamorous, less heralded sister. Manly was Dannii to Bondi's Kylie.

For some time, Manly has used a slogan to advertise itself: 'seven miles from Sydney, a thousand miles from care'. Visitors have taken those words to heart, and since 2000, Manly has become a backpacker mecca, as travellers finally discovered there was a beach in Sydney that wasn't called Bondi. It achieved major billing in the august pages of the travellers' Bible—the *Lonely Planet*. In fact, they described it as 'the jewel of the North Shore'.

Daytrippers would come over for a surf and never leave. Suddenly every waitress seemed to be from Surrey or Sao Paulo, Prague or Toronto. They realised that they could live in a place where the living was easy, the sky was big and blue every day, the surf was on one side, the harbour on the other, and joining the two was a pedestrian corso (imaginatively named The Corso), along which there were four drinking establishments and two bottle shops.

There were big backpacker hostels sprouting up around the town centre, and if you met a few like-minded souls in the first week, then there were plenty of fleapit two-bedroom apartments within a 2-minute stumble to the waves—and being backpackers, two bedrooms means dividing the rent with four, five, or 12 others. Surely this was paradise.

To get to the centre of Sydney from Manly is one of the least unpleasant commutes known to man, a half-hour ride on a ferry across one of the world's most scenic harbours. Manly residents often bitch about the ferries. This is because they are often cancelled without notice or explanation. They completely stop around midnight, even though many people on the Manly side of the harbour don't have evil stepsisters, and thus like to do things in the city after the clock strikes 12. And the fares keep going up with no perceived improvement in service, although at just over six bucks, it's surely the cheapest harbour cruise on the planet, taking in two of this country's icons—the Harbour Bridge and the Opera House.

Normally, if the swell isn't too big, there's no strike action being undertaken that day, and no boats have accidentally crashed into anything, you can consult your timetable, get there 5 minutes before departure, grab a coffee, casually stroll on board, and take in the view for half an hour.

Of course, laden with a backpack and keen to get to Bondi and get this book started, I arrived at the wharf to find a queue that stretched 50 metres from the gate, snaking back past the newsagent, the gelato stand, and spilling out onto the forecourt. Nobody explained why. Which was normal.

And right in front of me, there he was. The first whingeing Pom of my journey. We were in for a long wait, but he had a long list of grievances, so the whingeing was seemingly without end. He was talking to his friend, who it took me 15 minutes to ascertain was Australian, because he didn't get a chance to speak for that long.

The Englishman was reminiscent of the character in the movie *American Pie,* who could endlessly tell stories that began with the phrase, 'This one time, at band camp...'

Instead, the whingeing Pom would start each story with 'In England...'

'In England, the beer tastes so much better than here.'

If that's the case, I thought, then why do you people drink your body weight in our inferior beer every day that you're here?

'In England, it's not as expensive as it is here.'

Oh please. London is one of the most expensive cities on earth. Sydney isn't cheap, but as our dollar is like the peso compared to the English pound, you screw us in the exchange rate.

'In England, the cab drivers have to do a test called the knowledge, so they never get lost like your cab drivers do.'

This, even I admit, is true. But the fact he was travelling in taxis indicated that he wasn't exactly slumming it as a backpacker.

'In England, we have real seasons.'

Oh yes. There's that long, cold, wet season, followed by that other long, cold, wet season. Then the sun comes out for a fortnight, and everyone complains about the heat. Then there's another long, cold, wet season. The consistent sunshine and endless blue sky of Sydney is, admittedly, a predictable bore for the UK traveller.

His Australian companion, who I assumed was either in a hypnotic trance, or suffering from Stockholm syndrome, just nodded and smiled at everything his companion said.

Meanwhile, the line was moving a metre every 5 minutes. Perhaps, I thought to myself, this is what hell will be like. Or worse, maybe this is what the next month will be like.

When we finally got to Circular Quay on the other side of the harbour, the English guy was still listing the many advantages his home country had over the one he was standing in. As I made my way towards the bus stands, and he and his hapless buddy peeled away in the opposite direction, he was touting the superiority of the Penguin chocolate biscuit over the Tim Tam, a fool's argument in anyone's book. Especially mine. And so I went in search of a 380 bus.

I don't think I'm overstating the case when I say that the 380 is Satan's chariot on the highway to hell. Just about no one has a prepaid ticket on the 380. Just about everyone has an accent. You're only guaranteed of a seat if you're the driver. Each bus stop along the length and width of Hyde Park, the maddeningly congested stretch of Oxford Street, and the aimless dogleg route through Bondi Junction, is like another circle of purgatory, as Beelzebub's buggy gets waylaid for another 10 minutes while destinations are discussed, fares assessed, money (which is never at hand) is found, change is given, and luggage is stored.

There used to be a sign at the front of every Sydney bus

that read: 'Please do not talk to driver while bus is in motion'. On the 380 the sign should read: 'Driver will not shut up while bus is in motion'.

Our driver was what people my parents' age would call a 'character' and what people my age call 'a bit of a pain in the arse'. He commented on other drivers (judgement: useless), he commented on traffic (judgement: terrible, and getting worse by the year), he commented on the temperature (judgement: bloody hot), he gave a German mother detailed instructions on how she should stow her stroller, and he asked (at the top of his lungs) which film was playing at the outdoor cinema at Moore Park that evening.

'*Little Miss Sunshine*!' someone called out from halfway down the bus.

'*Little Ray Of Sunshine*?' he asked.

'*Little*! *Miss*! *Sunshine*!' a chorus of voices answered.

'Okay! Okay! No need to shout! Anyway, enjoy!' he shouted, before opening the doors so the cinema-goers could disembark.

At Bondi Junction he started cracking up and then pointed to a side street. There was a bedraggled looking bloke in his twenties, leaning flush against the side of a building, his fly undone, taking a piss.

'Must be a hole in the wall!' our driver yelled, doubling up with laughter.

The closer we got to our destination, the more surreal things seemed to become. A month later—well it seemed that long, okay?—we got to Bondi Beach.

I disembarked at the first stop at the southern end of the beach. It was very late in the afternoon, but the air was hot, wet, and salty, and the beach was still littered with bodies. The smell of fish and chips wafted from a nearby café, mixed with the whiff of suntan lotion and the fumes from the constant stream of cars that cruise up and down Campbell Parade, the promenade that runs along Sydney's most well-known stretch of sand and waves.

I found myself standing outside a building that was covered in a mural featuring whales and dolphins. I'm not generally a fan of murals featuring whales and dolphins, but I would have to get used to this one, as inside was my new home, a multi-level backpacker hostel called Noah's, that housed 250 travellers. At the front desk I paid my $32 and was handed a swipecard on a blue lanyard, which I was certainly not going to be hanging around my neck. I still had some dignity at this early stage. That would soon be gone.

I trudged upstairs, found my room number, swiped my card in the lock, opened the door, and there it was—a square room approximately 5 metres along each side, accommodating four double-decker bunks and just enough space for the floor to be evenly covered with empty beer bottles, wine casks, odd (and odd-smelling) socks, decaying food, and the spilled-out contents of seven backpacks. There were two windows set in one wall, eight small lockers packed against another, and a ceiling fan.

Submitting to the backpacker lifestyle means giving up your solitude and your personal space, and the dimensions and layout of the dorm room work towards making this a reality. I made my way through the detritus on the floor and found an empty bunk, where I dumped my pack and promptly laid down next to it. None of my room-mates were in, but my eyes and my nose gave me a mental picture of who they might be. I took a deep breath and detected a smell that was a beguiling combination of sweat, foot odour, body odour, farts, mildew, stale alcohol, cigarette smoke, and a faint bottom note of cheap perfume (perhaps a couple of girls had recently stayed in the room).

On the window ledge was a pair of those small, cheap speakers that can be hooked up to an MP3 player. I tried to imagine what had last been blasted through them at such volume levels that they distorted—Oasis? Jack Johnson? Bad hip-hop? Bad Europop? Sorry, bad Europop is a tautology.

I could see books on two different beds, and was encouraged to note that only one of them was Dan Brown's *The Da Vinci Code*. Unfortunately, on closer inspection, the other one proved to be Dan Brown's *Angels & Demons*.

There were also three copies of the *Lonely Planet* guide to Australia, but I would put money on the other four people in the room having copies on their person right at that moment. I know that I had mine with me. Backpackers refer to this book as the Bible and they follow what it says religiously. That gave me an idea. I got out my notebook, propped myself against the wall and decided to write down some rules for this trip.

1) I have to stay in a shared dorm room. Would I prefer to have a room by myself? Of course. But I needed to be there

at three in the morning when someone pisses out the window next to my head, turns on the lights to yell 'Where's my passport?' over and over again, sings 'Wonderwall' with the aid of a chronically out-of-tune acoustic guitar, or sobs until sunrise because their 'boyfriend' (who they met three days ago) has left them for some slutty Canadian.

2) No flying. No car. I have to 'ride the dog'—take the Greyhound bus. This will take longer, will be more frustrating, and will be insanely more uncomfortable, but it will bring me into contact with fellow travellers who are also living on a budget.

3) I have to say yes, whether this is to doing something stupid, illegal, carnal or toxic.

4) I will follow the Bible wherever possible, from its recommendations on food to accommodation to sights.

I opened up the Bible, and there on page 30 was my itinerary mapped out for me—the four-week east coast run. I'd heard that everyone follows this trail like a line of sunburnt, hungover ants, from Sydney to Byron Bay to Hervey Bay and Fraser Island, to Airlie Beach and the Whitsundays, and finally to Cairns. I wanted the backpacker experience, I needed to be an ant.

As there was no point sitting in an empty room, and the sun was starting to sink below the horizon, this little ant got himself together and went downstairs to The Shack.

*   *   *

The Shack, which was attached to the hostel, was trying its best to be a ramshackle little beach bar, but due to a combination of the clientele and the atmosphere, it came across as a miniature beer barn or a bad English holiday pub.

That night's entertainment revolved around a pool competition, with the blaring tunes (Fergie's 'London Bridge', Justin's 'SexyBack', an interminable live version of Queen's 'Bohemian Rhapsody' that seemed to run twice as long as the original) regularly interrupted by a tubby English girl with curiously orange skin who was acting as MC for the evening.

She used a microphone, but seemed unaware of the fact that this piece of technology actually amplified one's voice, so she yelled into it. She was also inordinately fond of the word 'Orrriiight'.

'Orrriiight! Do you wanna toss the boss? Get to it then! Orrriiight!'

'Orrriiight! Congrats to Damo for winning the pool competition! You get a six-pack of beer or a bottle of wine! Orrriiight!'

'Orrriiight! G'bye and good luck to Pete! It's been a great six months, mate! You take care, Pete! Orrriiight? Orrriiight!'

By that point, after a couple of beers and a chicken schnitzel that had the consistency of shoe leather, I was not feeling 'orrriiight' and was thinking of moving on. But then I met Camille.

She was tall, sultry and French, which are three qualities that make it difficult to leave a bar. She was sitting at the other end of my bench in deep discussion with a good-looking guy. Then he left to get drinks or go to the bathroom or something. She turned to me and said hi, and in the first 60 seconds, without my asking, explained that the guy was not her boyfriend.

I looked around for hidden cameras. Surely this was some sort of set-up.

She was from Paris, where she worked as a tour guide on a boat that cruised along the Seine. But she wanted to be an air hostess for Air France.

'All I want to do is travel,' she said. 'I want adventure in my life. Are you here for adventure also?'

I swear, this is how she really talked.

'Yes, I'm here for adventure also,' I replied. For some reason I was adopting her speech patterns and sounding like English was my second language.

'I think you are from England, yes?'

'No! That's like me saying you're from Belgium.'

She laughed. And it wasn't even a good joke.

I explained that I was from Australia.

'And what do you do, Mr Australian?'

'I'm a writer. Actually, I'm writing about backpackers. That's why I'm here. Maybe I'll get your story.'

'A writer? Interesting.'

She shifted closer to me on the bench. Contrary to what TV shows such as *Californication* may suggest, I've always found that telling a woman I'm a writer makes her move further away from me. Perhaps it's because I bear very little resemblance to David Duchovny. Anyway, all of a sudden I was feeling orrriiight. And a little stunned.

Her friend exhibited impeccable timing by coming back with drinks, and introductions were made. If he was any more of a French stereotype he would have had to be carrying a baguette and wearing a beret and a striped shirt with a nametag attached to it that read 'Gerard Depardieu'. He answered one of my questions with a shrug and the other with three words, none of which I understood. Then he sulked. Then he said he was going to play pool, and left the table.

'His girlfriend is coming over here in two days' time,' Camille explained, making that exhaling sound through vibrating lips, an expression that French girls always seem to use in order to convey exasperation.

I nodded, but secretly wondered what kind of mood he'd have been in if his girlfriend *wasn't* coming over here in two days' time. Maybe it was a French thing.

'I came to Australia by myself,' she continued. 'And I met him here at the hostel.'

Do you like travelling by yourself?

'Of course. I like to do my own thing. I'm an independent woman. I don't like staying in the one place. I am a person who likes the adventures.'

Yes, the adventures.

'I have lots of little dreams. When I was seven years old I told my mother that I wanted to live in New York. And I said I wanted to go to Los Angeles and touch the Hollywood sign.

These things will happen if you just believe. I wanted to come to Australia, and now here I am.'

Jesus. She was speaking like she was in a movie. In fact, she was speaking exactly like Julie Delpy in *Before Sunrise*, the 1995 Richard Linklater film where a twentysomething French girl (Delpy) and a twentysomething American guy (played by Ethan Hawke) meet on a European train, make a connection, and decide to get off in Vienna and spend one night walking around, talking incessantly about life, and falling for each other in the process. Just like Delpy's character, Camille seemed to be idealistic, open-hearted, naive, and wide-eyed. No cynicism, no limits. But I was no Ethan Hawke. That sense of possibility starts shrinking as you get older. You experience stuff, you start seeing the angles, you think three steps ahead, you contain yourself, you get realistic, you worry about consequences.

'I must go.'

Sorry?

'I must go. I must meet a friend. But you are still here tomorrow night, yes?'

Yes, I am.

'I am here at half past seven tomorrow, to eat. I cannot wait later than this to eat. I get *very* hungry.'

Um. Okay. I might see you then...then.

'Barry.'

Yes?

'Barry. This is your name, yes?'

Yes.

'Goodnight.'

I remembered about three things from high school French, and one of them was how to say 'see you soon'.

'*A bientot*,' I said.

She smiled.

'*A bientot*, Barry.'

Merde. What just happened?

After my new French friend vanished into the night, I went for a walk along Campbell Parade for an hour. A friend who lives in Bondi told me that his buddies call this 'The Gaza Strip'. Although I'm sure most Palestinians living in the real thing would disagree with the comparison, there was a certain wasteland quality to the main drag late at night. There was still activity, but the fluorescent-lit takeaway shops, the cram-'em-in outdoor restaurants that offer full English breakfasts, the groups of sun-reddened, hazy-eyed, people weaving drunkenly on the footpath, the line of ragged punters jostling to get into the sweaty Hotel Bondi, the line of better-heeled punters jostling to get into the more upmarket Ravesi's bar, and the thick-necked hoons revving their souped-up Japanese cars along the road, were not the kinds of things you tended to see on Bondi postcards.

I got back to my room after midnight, and even before I was through the door, I could hear loud voices, but they appeared to be speaking in another language. I walked in and the heat and the smell of alcohol was overpowering. Four heads swung around, all red and shiny, all topped with short, gelled, sweaty hair.

'Horp yeff broate bears wit ya or ya nort coomin uhn ere mairt.'

Sorry?

'Ah set, horp yeff broate bears wit ya or ya nort coomin uhn ere.'

I laughed. I had absolutely no idea what this guy was saying to me. Then it clicked: hope you've brought beers with you or you're not coming in here.

They were Irish. They were drunk. I would either need a translator, or they would have to say everything four times before I understood. To aid their alcohol consumption, they were playing some sort of drinking game with a deck of cards. I watched for a while but couldn't ascertain exactly what the rules were, and I wasn't sure they were adhering to any of the rules anyway. A drinking game 'punishes' you by making you take a drink. This seems like a fatally flawed rule considering most people play drinking games to get drunk.

They offered me a beer from the carton of 24 on the floor. There was an empty slab discarded in the corner and the bin was brimming with empties. There was also a half-empty bottle of Jack Daniels. The game seemed to be winding down and they told me about themselves.

The leader of the group appeared to be Mick, who everyone referred to as The Buzzer. He wouldn't be drawn on his nickname. He looked to be in his early forties, his short black hair liberally flecked with grey, his face deeply lined, his eyes red and rheumy, his teeth yellow from nicotine. I found out later he was only 29.

'This is no lie, Baz,' he said. Within 60 seconds of introducing myself—as Barry—he was calling me Baz. 'We've only been here three days, and within 8 minutes of getting here at the hostel, we met three people we knew from back home. I love this place, man. I'm on a five-day bender, but then I'll have to get my hat on and look for work.'

He'd only brought 500 Euros with him. He was now down to his last 70 Australian dollars. He'd spent most of it on alcohol and ecstasy. The party started the minute the lads left home.

'We got the plane from Dublin to Heathrow, and then Heathrow to Dubai,' he said. 'The four of us drank every little bottle of Jack Daniels and vodka on those planes. They had to refuel in Dubai, and restock the alcohol.'

He started laughing. It was uncannily like the bronchial snigger of Muttley, the dog from late-1960s cartoon *The Wacky Races*.

'We got here after 24 hours in a plane, had four hours sleep to recharge the batteries, and we've been drinking ever since. That four hours is the only sleep I've had in three days. Someone's got to do it. You've got to create that buzz, y'know?'

Had they got out of the hostel to see any of the city?

'Been to the Beach Road Hotel and the Bondi Hotel last night. Australian girls are a bit stuck up though, aren't they? I mean, I could do with an overhaul, but no luck. I was just going up to 'em and saying, 'Come on, let's have a pash'. No luck. No luck at all. And I'm just a train of love, you know what I mean?'

I had absolutely no idea what he meant, but I smiled and nodded anyway.

Quite unexpectedly he then started making beatbox noises with his mouth and commenced half-rapping, half-singing a song in a croaky baritone, like a cross between Barry White and Shane MacGowan.

'Baby, baby, if only my love could reach that far/Come with me on the boom-boom-boom train of love/choo choo Thomas the Tank Engine said/ch-ch-choo-choo, ch-ch-choo-choo, ch-ch-choo-choo, ch-ch-choo-choo/Baby, baby, if only my love could reach that far/Come with me on the boom-boom-boom train of love.'

A career as a Lothario-type character with The Wiggles (Lieutenant Lovepants, perhaps?) obviously awaited him, which would have made a nice change from his actual gigs at home—supermarket worker, flower seller, and gravedigger.

As more alcohol was consumed and the time dragged on from one to two to three o'clock in the morning, the lads got harder to understand, if that was possible. At one point I just let my tape recorder run, and right now I'll try to transcribe phonetically one of their exchanges. For context's sake, you should know that one of the lads' feet smelled like a particularly well-matured French cheese, and the others were taking some joy in pointing out this fact.

– Fer fook's sairk, poot yer shoes beck on.

– Fookin stinks, y'barstard.

– Foorty books fer the tuxi. We got screwed cos a'you.

– I ended oop in soomwoon else's baird but I cairn't tell ya boot it. Ah'd have t'kill ya.

– She reckon's he's shit in bed.

– Ah down give a fook whut she saird. And fook you too.

– Rog's flyin in tuh Brisbane at half sairven.

– Dead on. But ee wornt mairk ut. E's still pissed frum last nairt.

– We're not gawn till Wednesday moaning, thank God.

(The guy with the smelly feet starts scratching his back against the locker like a large bear)

– Smairly feet! Scratchy back! Fook ya!

– Gairt those feet awair from me bed y'fook!

– Would you shoot oop y'cryin bairstards!

– Oi've spairnt fifty books t'day and air've got nothin boot shrapnel.

– Jaysus, Paddy! Shoot oop wit ya whinin and gairt fooked.

At around 3:30, things quietened down a little. Nathan, a portly 30-year-old with curly hair and a sweet disposition, joined me where I was sitting on the windowsill, and lit up a cigarette. I didn't notice whether he'd been drinking less than his companions, but he definitely seemed more sober, and when he spoke I was relieved to find that I could understand nearly everything he said.

'You picked the right room, didn't you?' he said. 'I can't even believe I'm here. This fella here, Mick, called me on the phone on Saturday night and wanted me to go out. In Dublin everyone does a lot of coke all the time, so we were out all night and we got talking about Australia, and one thing led to another, and we decided to come here.'

'You're saying that this time last week, you had no idea you'd be coming here?' I asked.

'Too right. And Tuesday we're on the plane. I didn't have a cent in my pocket, either. This bloke's brother lent me a few grand. Otherwise I couldn't have done it.'

'How long are you here for?'

'Only three weeks. The others are staying longer though. They've got work visas.'

He got quiet for a moment and we both looked out the window for a while. A girl across the street was wildly swinging a cricket bat and finding this so amusing that she couldn't stop laughing.

'This is my last blaze of glory,' he finally said. 'I have two kids. Two little girls, three and seven. I'm not with their mother anymore because of my drinking. When I get home I'm giving up completely. My kids are the only things I miss out here. When I get home it's back to normality and trying to be a proper father.'

'What are you two talkin' about like little love birds?' Mick slurred from his bunk. 'Baz! Riddle me this! At the pub, how can you tell which girls are English?'

I had to admit I didn't know.

'They're the ones sitting in the corner smoking pipes!'

Mick loved this joke so much that he had a coughing fit. Ten minutes later he was so dead to the world that even one of his mate's smelly shoes, gently placed over his nose and photographed with much glee, were not enough to wake him.

The next morning I woke up early. Well, early for a backpacker. This means I roused myself before the crack of noon. I decided to go for a swim. Despite the fact it was early January, the middle of the Australian summer, it was uncharacteristically grey and blustery, there was only a scattering of beach-goers for a Sunday, and the water was so cold that I soon lost all feeling in my lower half. Although I have no desire to father children, at that moment it felt like I would no longer have a choice in the matter.

I went for breakfast at a café in Hall Street, which runs perpendicular to the beach, uphill from Campbell Parade. Some of the shop windows there proudly displayed signed black-and-white photos of a skinny blonde woman. Many of the native Bondi females sport radar-dish sized sunglasses and miniscule skirts or shorts, and this 'fashion' owes a hell of a lot to the woman in those photos—Paris Hilton.

The air-headed heiress had visited Bondi the week before, and every commercial TV news bulletin that day carried footage of a moving scrum of people slowly shifting along the sand as she made her way into the water. Hilton played the bimbo to the hilt, emerging from the surf to coquettishly say that she'd forgotten to bring a towel (no mention was made of her brain). A gallant local handed his over, and after drying herself she handed it back and said (rather wittily, I thought, even as I simultaneously groaned at it) that he should put it on ebay. One thing is certain—Paris knows what she's worth, even if she doesn't have any particular talent.

While waiting for breakfast I perused the café noticeboard that was crowded with travellers' scrawled homemade advertisements for accommodation and cars. My two favourites:

1989 Laser. This is a perfect car whom has served me well for some time and never let me down. She has to go because I am now leaving Australia. I am sad to leave both the country and the car, as she is like a family to me now. Minor beauty damages and left passenger window will not open (easy to fix!).
Call Jakob.

ROOM AVAILABLE IN BONDI
Class house.
Must be cool.
No stress-heads.
Must like dogs.
Girls preferred.
Call Jon or Steve.

I had some empathy with Jakob's heartfelt advertisement. I'm the owner of a 1989 Laser myself, and one does tend to get attached to them, with their rust outbreaks, ghostly rattles, random leaks and subsequent mouldy smell after heavy rain. It is a car that is hard to kill however, so whoever ended up purchasing this little beauty should be rest-assured that, as Elton John almost said, the chassis will rust out long before the engine ever dies.

I could picture Jon and Steve's house, as their ad was a very clever series of coded messages. Please allow me to translate:

Class house—a 24-hour party place.

In Bondi—in Bondi Junction, on a main road, above a kebab shop, and nowhere near the beach.

No stress-heads—you are disqualified if you ever like to sleep before 3 a.m. or have to work the next day.

Must like dogs—inside the house is carpeted with dog hair; outside it is carpeted with dog shit.

Girls preferred—we haven't had sex for a long while because we're crap at chatting up girls, so if a couple of chicks moved in, it would make things a whole lot easier, especially if you were German or Swedish, because we wouldn't even have to go out to try to pick up, as you'd bring all your girlfriends round, and it would be like a babe smorgasbord. Also, you may like to do the washing-up (which was last done in 2004) and find the vacuum cleaner (which Jon's mum bought us sometime around the Olympics, but we can't seem to find it anywhere) and give it a run around the place, because this dog hair is even starting to give us the shits.

That night I'm aware that Camille is getting to The Shack at 7:30 because, if you remember, 'I cannot wait later than this to eat. I get *very* hungry'.

I displayed great restraint and, if I don't say so myself, inner reserves of laissez-faire by turning up at 7:35.

She was sitting at a table, smoking a cigarette and drinking a beer with a guy, but not her French companion from the night before. She didn't see me, and I didn't feel like going straight up to her. I felt awkward so I went to buy a beer and some time. I hung at the bar for a little while, felt more awkward, and then thought, 'Jesus, this is ridiculous. You're not 15. Just go up and say hi.'

'Hi,' I said as casually as I could. She was wearing a diaphanous top that plunged down her back. She was wearing tight black jeans and heels.

'Oh, hi...Brad?' she said.

Wow. This was going well.

'Um, Barry.'

'Barry! Yes. Barry.'

As someone will tell me in an hour's time, French girls never say sorry. She introduces me to her companion, a Belgian called Kenneth. Like other Belgians I'd met in my travels, when he spoke I immediately thought of the strange, sing-song cadences of the old children's TV puppet show *Bill*

& Ben. He had curly brown hair, an impish grin, and a tendency to monopolise the conversation.

After about 10 minutes Camille said that she had to go and meet her French friend, and she had to eat.

'Because you get *very* hungry,' I said.

'I told you this?'

Jesus, she couldn't remember our conversation at all. She left me with Kenneth, and we ended up talking until three in the morning.

Or rather, he ended up talking until three in the morning and I just tried to keep up with the note-taking for the first half hour, and then told him I was going to have to grab my tape recorder. He had quite a story to tell. Kenneth was one of the happiest people I have ever met, and a week ago he lost just about everything he owned.

Ever since he was a boy, Kenneth wanted to come to Australia. *Neighbours* was big in Belgium, and he became fascinated with a place that had so much sunshine and so much bad acting.

When he left school be became a long-distance truck driver in Europe, started socking away money, and finally, on 16 January 2006, he landed in Sydney. His first impression wasn't good. Where were the wide open spaces, the gum trees, and the kangaroos? Sydney just felt like another city to him. So he travelled down to Melbourne with a Dutch guy he met in the hostel. Kenneth doesn't have trouble meeting people. He will talk to anyone.

He stayed in Melbourne for a while and bought a Toyota Lite Ace van. By this time he had met a French girl and they decided to travel together along the Great Ocean Road towards Adelaide. The two would always end up having 'discussions', a word Kenneth uses four times until I realise he actually means 'arguments'.

'Whether I was parking the van or deciding what to make for dinner, there would always be a half-hour discussion,' he said. 'She was annoying.'

And you were sleeping in the van every night?

'Yes.'

With a French girl?

'Yes.'

And nothing happened?

'No.'

This is a very strange story.

'You obviously haven't met many French girls. What can I say? They're very narrow-minded and, as my father used to say, they must come with an instruction manual that none of us own.'

They parted ways in Adelaide and he immediately met a German couple. There were more 'discussions'.

'The guy was cool, but she was...how do you say it? A mama's child? A spoilt brat? If things didn't go her way she was pissed off. That caused a bit of discussion as well. We travelled towards Alice Springs for two weeks.'

What also caused a bit of 'discussion' was the fact that Kenneth encouraged the German guy to smoke pot with him.

For Kenneth, smoking was not a casual thing. It was a full-time occupation. He claimed, only half-jokingly, that he couldn't drive if he was straight. He bought an ounce of pot in Adelaide for $180 and by the time he got to William Creek, a dot on the map west of Lake Eyre, he'd run out. Ironically, William Creek is Australia's lowest point, and as Kenneth was in the middle of nowhere, and out of weed, he could relate.

Fortunately, the only thing that Kenneth can attract faster than fellow travellers is marijuana. Way out there in a town, which at the last census had an official population of 16, the first two guys he met were from Melbourne, and they had pot. Despite the fact they were 20 years older than Kenneth, they became fast friends.

So everyone was happy. No discussions. They eagerly agreed to go in convoy with Kenneth and the German couple, tagging along in their Suzuki four-wheel drive. By the time they got to Coober Pedy, they'd smoked all that weed as well.

They stopped for petrol in Coober Pedy and when Kenneth went in to pay he noticed that the young guy behind the counter had a pack of kingsize rolling papers.

'You wouldn't happen to know where I could get some green, would you?' he asked.

'Yeah, no worries, mate,' said his new friend.

He started making some calls and an hour later Kenneth had another ounce of weed. This time it cost $350. The price was going up, but let's face it, this was a supply and demand situation. He wasn't in Amsterdam or Nimbin.

When the convoy got to Alice Springs, Kenneth dropped the German couple at a hostel, and went to meet up with his Melbourne buddies in a parking area near the Todd River. And that's when he fell in love.

Two German girls were sitting in their car writing in their diaries. They were the most beautiful girls Kenneth had seen in Australia. He went straight up to them and introduced himself.

'I'm not shy,' Kenneth noted, quite unnecessarily at this point. 'After two hours of conversation I found out these girls liked drum and bass music. Now, I absolutely love drum and bass music. So I hooked up my iPod to my speakers and carried it in my backpack, and we went into town. We were walking around Woolworth's dancing to drum and bass in the middle of Alice Springs as if we were at a dance party.'

And no one beat you up or shot at you?

'No. They looked at us strangely, but that's alright.'

Were you stoned?

'Well, yeah. I was always stoned at that time.'

Kenneth didn't want to leave the girls, and he had fallen pretty heavily for one of them, a blonde 23-year-old from Berlin. But they were moving on to Townsville and he was running out of money and needed to work. Within two hours he'd found a job working on a cattle station. He had to catch cattle and help brand and castrate them. Kenneth had never worked on a farm before in his life and had trouble adjusting. He could feel the stress and terror of the animals as they were lined up. His job was to help pull the animals over onto their sides, then put all his weight on one hind leg of the bull, while pulling the other leg up so the farmer could castrate it. The bulls would defecate and urinate all over him. He was paid $400 a week, plus accommodation and meals.

'I hated it,' he said. 'I didn't like hurting the animals. I lasted two weeks. And I hated my boss, who was always pushing me to the limit. I'm an easy-going guy, but I'd had enough. So I said I couldn't work for him anymore. He pushed me and I nearly had a fight with him. I'm not even a good fighter, but I had to stand up to him.'

So he drove to Alice Springs and planned on driving to Townsville to follow his heart. How far is that?

'It's about a 50-spliff drive,' said Kenneth, with a big grin.

And here things really took a turn for the worse. I'd been amazed at his Dorothy-like journey down the yellow brick road so far, happily meeting people who could supply him with pot in the most out of the way places. That was about to change. In Alice he hooked up with a local who drove a hotted-up black Holden Commodore. He gave Kenneth his number and said to call the next day. An ounce would cost $400. The cost was rising again. He and his two Melbourne friends agreed to put in $200 each.

'I really didn't have a good feeling about it and I told him so when we met the next day. The guy said, 'Look, I'll give you my mobile phone. I'll take the money, I'll drive towards the highway, turn left, and then I'll be back in 10 minutes.'

Kenneth agreed. The guy drove off. Ten minutes passed. Then another ten. Then another ten. Kenneth was not happy.

The two Melbourne guys, when Kenneth called them to tell them what had happened, were even less so. Kenneth had the guy's phone, but he soon discovered that the simcard had been taken out. So, Mr Commodore still had his simcard, but Kenneth had his name and number, and had written down his car registration. He dialled the number all day with no luck. At six o'clock, Mr Commodore finally answered. Words were exchanged.

'Listen,' said Kenneth. 'You don't want to fuck around with a Belgian guy. I want my weed or I want my money back. You might be a local, but I am pissed off and I will hunt you down.'

'Mate, you are full of shit,' replied Mr Commodore. 'Meet me at the Coles parking lot in 15 minutes and I will kick the shit out of you.'

Kenneth showed. The guy didn't. There were more phone calls. In a scene from some 1950s gang movie, they met later that night on ANZAC Hill in Alice Springs. Kenneth was with one of his friends from Melbourne, who was built like a wrestler. But Mr Commodore had arrived with three mates. Kenneth suspected he would be outnumbered, which is why he had decided to carry a machete. As soon as Mr Commodore pulled up, Kenneth pulled out the machete and started beating the car with it. This took Mr Commodore unawares, so he sped off, tyres squealing and throwing up blue smoke in the parking lot.

Kenneth and his Melbourne mountain-man gave chase along the Stuart Highway. Kenneth had driven trucks all his life and has a lead foot, so he quickly caught up with the Commodore, but they started throwing stubbies out the window to try to blow Kenneth's tyres. This went on for an hour-and-a-half. Then Kenneth ran out of petrol. And he realised that he wasn't going to get his money or his weed.

Now he really felt like a smoke. He was so indignant that he went to the police station and reported Mr Commodore.

'I gave this guy $400 to buy weed from him, and he ripped me off,' Kenneth explained to the cops. 'Look, I have his name, his phone number and his car registration.'

Apparently the officers on duty kept straight faces while telling him they could be of no help whatsoever in this situation. So Kenneth drove to Townsville—a 50-spliff drive with no weed—and met up with the German girl again.

'I never got it on with her,' he says. 'But she is like one of my soulmates. I'm still in contact with her and I hope one day something will happen with us.'

Kenneth found a job harvesting sugar cane in Ayr, about 90 kilometres south of Townsville. He earned around $1500 a week, but he was working seven days a week, harvesting between 800 and 1000 tonnes of sugar cane a day, from 4:30 in the morning to seven at night. In just over two months he'd saved $10,000, and moved on for some rest and recreation in Cairns, where he proceeded to spend $3000 in two weeks.

'It was time to relax,' he said with a shrug. 'I'd never worked so hard in my life.'

What did he spend the money on?

'Pot, drinking, bungee jumping, skydiving. It was all worth it, believe me.'

He then slowly made his way down the east coast, tripping on LSD at a rainforest dance party outside Cairns, chilling out at Mission Beach, travelling to Airlie Beach with a German who looked like Arnold Schwarzenegger, spending three days on a boat in the Whitsundays, finding out he loved double vodka and Red Bull in Hervey Bay, and finding out they didn't really mix with driving when he almost crashed a four-wheel drive on Fraser Island.

'On Fraser Island I learned that English girls are the way forward.'

What do you mean?

'They know how to drink, they know how to party, and they do like their one-night stands.'

He got to Byron Bay and naturally had to hang out in Nimbin for a while. He was sitting on a bench in the street smoking a joint when he noticed a pretty girl who was making various animal noises and pretending to swim on the concrete. She then walked up to Kenneth and literally fell into his arms. She looked into his eyes and said, 'I've got a bed full of oranges. Would like to come and see them?'

Kenneth did, but after aimlessly walking around with her for ages, and deciding that she was way too far into an acid trip, he said goodbye to her.

He drove to Sydney and got here on 28 December, only to discover that there wasn't a bed to be found in Bondi. No problem. He would sleep in his van. He parked in Coogee and went to meet a couple of friends in Kings Cross for some drinks. When he returned, the van was gone.

'I'm about to go to New Zealand so I was going to sell the van to get some money back. And just about everything I owned was in there—my backpack, my clothes, my iPod, my laptop, my passport. I lost it all.'

That's terrible.

'You know what? I wasn't really worried about it. I was like, "Okay, I've lost everything, but I'm still alive, I'm in Australia, I can still smile." It's only material things.

'Maybe Australians have taught me this laidback attitude. Before I came to Australia, I was obsessed with money. But from travelling in Australia I've learned that money isn't important. It's the state of mind you're in, the people that you know, and the memories that you have that are important. They're all worth more than ten thousand in your bank account if you're unhappy.'

Losing his van and his possessions was also a wake-up call.

'I decided to quit smoking weed. I'd been smoking so much that I was no longer in reality. I've probably smoked an ounce a week since I've been here, and I've been here a whole year. So I've smoked enough for the next five years anyhow.'

I told him that was quite a story.

'Yeah, my long-term memory's fine but my short-term memory's fucked.'

You can't remember my name, can you?

He looked at me sheepishly.

'I can't, I'm sorry.'

I re-introduced myself, four hours after we first met.

'It's been good speaking to you,' he said. 'You want another beer?'

I certainly did. I'd also completely forgotten about Camille, who I would never see again. As I wasn't in possession of the manual on how French women operated, it would have been pretty futile anyway.

I've decided to try to learn to surf. Emphasis on the word *try*. I'm pale. I'm unfit. My daily exercise regime is as follows—make sure coffee and newspapers are at least a 20-minute walk away from my office. That way I walk at least 40 minutes a day. Or if writers' block is particularly bad that day, I walk up to five hours a day. Those days are great for my cardiovascular system, and terrible for my bank balance.

I booked a lesson with a company in North Bondi. The very next day the surf was so big that the beach was closed. The forecast for the day of my lesson was for fresh winds on a big swell. I was starting to chicken out already.

I grew up around Manly Beach, and I was a keen bodysurfer in my teens and twenties, but my experiences on a surfboard were very limited. I tried to learn once when I was about 19. My teacher was a friend called Rip. He got his nickname not from the thing I feared most in the surf, but because his surname was McNaughton. The initial nickname was Rip Snortin' McNaughton, which got shortened to Rip Snortin', and thence to Rip.

He decided to teach his girlfriend to surf, and as he had an extra board, asked me along. Rather than taking us to a nice sheltered beach with small, gentle waves, Rip took us to Curl Curl, a treacherous place north of Manly on a cold, blustery day. He gave us a quick lesson in paddling then told us to follow him out the back. What felt like three days and 15 litres of swallowed seawater later, we were finally out beyond where the waves broke, sitting on our boards.

'I'll just catch a wave,' he told us, as saltwater monsters flecked with whitecaps periodically rolled beneath us. 'Then I'll come back and we'll start.'

He was gone on the next wave. Five minutes passed. Ten minutes. Fifteen minutes. Was this a bizarre teaching method that involved leaving the novices to their own devices? Was it a hilarious practical joke that would result in Rip losing a girlfriend either by drowning, or by her somehow making it to dry land and beating him to death with his own board?

His girlfriend and I decided that we should try to get back to the beach, which sounds like an easy thing to do, but in waves that big and with experience so small, this was no mean feat. On the beach, before we went into the water, Rip had taught us about waiting for the right wave and how they came in sets, so we hung around until the biggest wave went through, and caught one that wasn't quite so gargantuan, bodyboarding our way into shore.

And there was Rip, sitting on the sand with a red T-shirt wrapped around his foot. But he wasn't wearing a red T-shirt when we arrived. It was white with pale blue stripes. He'd been dumped and finned by his own board, opening up a gash in his ankle. We spent the remainder of the lesson in the emergency ward at Manly Hospital where Rip received five stitches and I formally retired from a budding surfing career. (By the way, although Rip's girlfriend didn't go on to become a pro-surfer either, they obviously got over this incident because she ended up marrying him, and as far as I know they're living happily ever after.)

I'd managed to avoid plunging into the ocean with a board ever since and could feasibly maintain this abstinence until the day I died. But I was meant to be a yes-man on this trip, and as two Israeli girls I'd met at The Shack were talking about giving it a try, and then said they'd do it if I did, we figured there'd be strength in numbers. The deal was sealed over tequila shots.

At three o'clock on a Thursday afternoon we wandered up the blistering hot boardwalk to North Bondi to the surf store, and within minutes I was being ordered to strip down to my budgie smugglers. I was then handed a damp wetsuit, topped off by a rash vest that was done out in a very fetching shade of iridescent pink.

There were 18 people to be divided up among two instructors—a half dozen Australians, along with a mix from

England, Germany, Japan, Canada, Israel and the United States. Our teacher was Julia, a wiry, sun-bleached local whose voice was still recovering from a bout of the flu. We walked down to the sand past hordes of beach-goers, and in my get-up I felt like I was auditioning for a new position in The Village People.

Julia dealt out boards, checking our height and asking about our previous experience before choosing one of appropriate length. I was relieved to discover that the boards were not fibreglass, but made of foam with a soft shell and rubbery fins. We did some warm-up exercises, then 15 minutes of instruction on the beach, where we emulated catching a wave. I stood up easily. Maybe that was not such a mean feat, as I was actually on sand, not water, but one of the English guys in our group was obviously working with a hangover and I noticed he had trouble keeping balance.

Then we paddled out into the white water. Julia was starting us off on broken waves to ease us into it. Where was she when Rip left me out the back at Curl Curl all those years ago?

It's harder to catch a wave than it looks. There's a lot of paddling involved, and it takes it out of you. After about 10 minutes my back and arms ached, and I was having trouble catching my breath.

The first time I tried to stand up, the board flew away to the left. Which would have been fine, except I flew away to the right.

I paddled out again. The second time I tried to stand up, I got a cramp in my right leg and fell backwards—the board travelled nicely on the wave, which I happened to be tumbling underneath at the time.

The third time I tried to get up, the board and I were going in the same direction, but as soon as I got to my feet, I felt a sudden sharp pain at the base of my spine, as if someone had jammed a hypodermic needle into my back. The pain was hot and electric and I stumbled to my knees, and rode the wave in on my stomach.

The fourth time I tried to get up...I actually did get up, albeit thanks to Julia holding the board in place, waiting for the right wave, then thrusting me forward with the following encouraging words, yelled at the top of her hoarse lungs: 'Paddle! Paddle! Paddle!' I did. I pushed down on the board at the right moment. I felt the wave suck me into it, then push me forward. I sprung to my feet. I got up. I stayed up. I was so wrapped that even as the wave started to lose power, I didn't want to get off so I kept going. And finally I flipped off the board, landing with a wet slap in around 30 centimetres of water, right at the feet of a pretty girl who was walking in the shallows.

'Did that hurt?' she asked, with a slight grin.

'Yes,' I answered. 'But I only did it to impress you.'

After 10 minutes in the water I felt like quitting. After an hour-and-a-half I didn't want to stop.

One of my Israeli friends, a tall, sturdy girl with long black hair and a big smile, took to the surf as if she'd been doing it forever. The other, who was petite, freckled and a little standoffish, seemed to hate every minute of it, and ended up sitting on the beach for the second half of the lesson.

'That was a complete waste of money,' she grumbled when we returned to the sand.

'What'd you come to Australia for then?' asked the English guy, who had not only recovered from his hangover, but was bucking the stereotype by not joining her in whingeing.

According to Tourism Research Australia, each backpacker spends around $5000 in Australia, which is twice as much as other tourists. This isn't so much because they're loaded, but because they hang around a lot longer. Research shows that the average stay is two months for a backpacker—as opposed to one month for regular tourists—but I met many who were measuring their trips by the year. Altogether they pour $2.3 billion a year into the economy. And surely a lot of that must go on alcohol.

If I were a Bondi businessman, I'd open a bottle shop opposite a hostel. The holiday snaps of the typical Bondi backpacker do not include the Opera House, the Harbour Bridge or cute koalas and kangaroos at Taronga Park Zoo. No, their digital cameras are full of images of themselves and others just like them in various stages of inebriation. Their life here is circumscribed by the hostel, the strip of beach at the end of the hostel's street, and the pubs around the corner from the hostel. They don't meet many Australians, unless those Australians happen to be standing behind the bar and it is necessary to communicate with them in order to obtain alcohol.

Back in January 2006, when I was spending my week in Bondi to write the magazine story, the hostel manager was a lanky, baby-faced 20-year-old Englishman named Liam. He told me that on the day before they have to go back home, he often saw backpackers desperately racing out to go to the city for a few hours to get some touristy pics to show mum and dad.

He ran me through the weekly social schedule at the hostel that kept them so busy. Monday was pizza night. Tuesday was movie and popcorn night. Wednesday was punch night, which involved everyone throwing in five dollars, and then inhaling a sweet, lethal cocktail of seven casks of wine, three bottles of vodka and fruit juice, mixed in one of those big plastic recycling bins. Thursday was karaoke night. Friday was another punch night and then into the city to visit a club or three. Saturday was a barbecue. And Sunday was live R&B at the Beach Road Hotel.

This was the official schedule. But unofficially everyone got legless in the courtyard and at the big communal table in the kitchen area from about five or six in the afternoon. They played poker, danced, flirted, played drinking games, and imbibed slabs of beer and cheap cask wine.

At about ten p.m., after getting well lubricated, the backpackers start weaving their way to the Beach Road Hotel a few blocks away. Wednesday night is the big night for backpackers at Bondi pubs, but in reality every night is party night. Sometime after midnight, when the Beach Road closes, they take a 15-minute stumble (it's a brisk 5-minute walk when sober) to the Hotel Bondi, where the place is vacuum-packed with sweaty, heaving bodies, and there are more accents than a United Nations summit.

At around four a.m., the faithful somehow navigate their way back to the hostel where many will continue their revelry until six in the morning. They catch up on a little sleep after that, their skin glowing red and peeling off in sheets, their bodies sweating pure alcohol, their clothes reeking of cigarette smoke. They have a late breakfast around lunchtime, covering most of the major food groups with instant coffee and a cigarette. They go for a surf and lie on the beach for a few hours. They have a late lunch with the first beers of the day. Maybe take a late afternoon nap. Have a shower. Buy the evening's alcohol supplies from the local bottle shop in Hall Street. Return to the hostel courtyard. Repeat.

At the risk of sounding like one of those old fogeys who sits in the corner smoking a pipe and telling stories that all start with the phrase 'Back in my day...', well, back in my day, hostels were very, very different. This was in the mid-to-late 1980s, when I was travelling around the United Kingdom.

For a start, the dorms were strictly same-sex affairs. On that first day in the Bondi hostel in 2006, after I was given my key and climbed the stairs to find my room, I opened the door and there were three girls sitting on the floor. Two of them were clothed and the other wore just a bra and a towel around her waist.

'Sorry!' I blurted. 'I think I've got the wrong room.'

'Which room were you after?' asked the girl in the bra and towel, who made no attempt to cover up.

'Two?' I said uncertainly.

'You're here,' said one of her friends. 'There's a spare bed over there on top of my bunk.'

I remember severe hostel wardens 20 years ago who would literally sneak around in the middle of the night with torches to check that no one had smuggled a girl into the men's dorms. Now they actually flung us together in the same room as a matter of course.

And then there were the hostel hours of old. Everyone had to be out of the place by eleven in the morning, and you couldn't return until after four in the afternoon. The place was locked up after everyone was herded out each morning, but it was just assumed that no one would want to hang around during the day. You were expected to be out and about, climbing hills, or visiting museums, or riding bikes, or wandering the countryside, or having informative discussions about castles with eccentric locals.

There was also a lights-out policy at night. I recall watching *Psycho* on TV one evening in a Scottish hostel with a bunch of other backpackers, and the warden pulled the plug at 11:30 p.m., despite our protests that the film only had 20 minutes left to go. Scottish hostel wardens were an especially tough breed. I'm pretty sure they were recruited from the Scottish penal system.

And then there were the chores. Yes, every person in the

place was given a daily job to do, from sweeping the hallways to raking the leaves to doing the washing up to cleaning the toilets, and you were expected to front up in the morning to perform this task and get your name marked off the list.

Every backpacker back then had a little plastic folder with their official Youth Hostel Association card inside, and each hostel had an individual stamp, often depicting a picture of a local landmark or a stylised rendering of the hostel itself. It was a point of pride to show other travellers all the stamps you'd amassed over a quiet beer in a local pub, after you'd met in the hostel kitchen earlier cooking up your vegetables and rice (yes, we all seemed to cook our own food as well). Tales would ensue about your adventures, hardships, discoveries, close shaves, and you'd swap tips about towns and hostels to visit or avoid.

And yes, I'm quite aware that all of this seems as quaint and archaic as an Enid Blyton book. And I'm also aware that there also existed in 1980s London a place called Earls Court, where Foster's flowed in the streets and budget traveller hotels shook to the sound of revelling Australian accents, occasionally mine. So I will shut up.

The Bondi hostel I'd stayed in back in 2006 was Indy's, a sweatbox of a place on Hall Street. It had a capacity of 80 people, crammed into one floor of tightly-packed rooms, with the peak season overflow willing to even pay for a spot on the floor in the TV room. I had initially tried to book in there again for this trip but being early January, it was full. But I kept thinking about the place. Noah's was over three times larger, but apart from The Shack and the kitchen, there was no central place where people could casually hang out and inevitably mix with each other. It was just too big.

The things that were potentially infuriating about Indy's—the close quarters, the ever-present smell of stale alcohol, the noise, the inability to get away from anyone—were exactly what I needed to get more up close and personal and meet a cross-section of people. So I ventured back to Hall Street after three days in Bondi to check it out again.

It was no longer called Indy's. Now it had a smart logo that read Surfside Backpackers. They had a new security gate, a snazzy website and a sister hostel in Coogee. They were now a mini-franchise. Despite these attempts at updating its image, everyone still called it Indy's. I was soon to find out this was because nothing much had changed apart from the name.

I pressed the buzzer to get in the gate and then walked down the laneway to the reception area. It was closed even though it was meant to be open. That was a good sign. The level of professionalism was still the same.

The beauty of this place for my purposes was the back verandah with long picnic tables where everyone congregated. I walked out there, took a seat and within 20 minutes I'd met half the population.

The first person I spotted was Max, a 20-year-old Dutch guy who I recognised from when I was staying here 12 months ago. He hadn't left. I was taken aback by how he looked. Back then he was intense, talkative, and fresh-faced, but now he appeared drawn and haggard, with bum fluff on his chin and a cough that sounded like he was trying to expel some small dead animal he had inadvertently swallowed last week.

'I've been sick,' he told me when I asked how he was going. 'I'm recovering. I did ecstasy every day or two for a whole month.'

I presumed he was telling me this because he remembered me. But then I realised he had no idea who I was. A half hour later he finally twigged.

'You were here last year, weren't you?' he said, looking up from his book and pointing. 'You're the magazine writer. Funny story, man. I read it when it came out.'

From just sitting there for a short time, a cast of characters started materialising before my eyes. It was like *Big Brother*, backpacker style.

There was the stereotypical skinny, sunburnt, chain-smoking, morose English girl who complained about everything. There was the stereotypical fat, sunburnt, morose, chain-smoking English girl who complained about everything.

There was the older English guy with shaggy blond hair and a hangdog face, singing along to The Undertones on his iPod, and furtively checking out the girls.

There were two Aussie blokes from Melbourne, up in Sydney on a road trip and ready for a bit of partying.

There was the good-looking Dutch guy, who started talking to me as soon as I sat down—I could tell he was the alpha male of the group by the way the guys deferred to him and the girls sneaked glances at him.

And there were two alpha females—a Canadian called Megan, who was managing the hostel, and another Canadian, an African-American called Dora. Megan had dyed jet-black hair, multiple piercings and a bit of attitude. Dora wore a blue playsuit, which she rolled down to reveal a white bikini. She'd fixed herself a plate of pasta, parked herself next to me and offered me some. She fed me a forkful.

'Good, isn't it?' she asked. 'So who are you?'

Yes, this place was friendly. And when Megan finally opened the office I discovered there were a couple of vacancies. So I booked back in.

As I left to get my stuff from the other hostel, a bearish Canadian rolled in and started giving high-fives to everyone.

'Did any of you guys even leave the hostel yesterday?' he asked in a booming voice.

There was a lazy chorus of shaking heads.

He gave a double thumbs-up.

'Alriiiiiiight!' he said.

I was home.

I booked in, dumped my backpack in one more small square room with four double bunks in it, and went out the back again to sit on the verandah. I didn't move for the next 12 hours. It's a condition known as Indy's Inertia.

The first slab of beer was torn open at noon. The ashtrays were full by two. A joint came out at three. At four we were gathered around a mobile phone, on which there was footage under the heading 'Kristin pissed'. A pale English girl with eyes so unfocused they appeared to be going in separate directions, was on the floor between two beds. She repeatedly tried to get up and repeatedly failed to. She kept falling backwards, collapsing into fits of laughter and screeching words that didn't appear to be in English. When she did finally get to her feet, she swayed unsteadily for a few seconds, then fell forward, her face taking up the whole screen, her mascara running, her face red and blotchy.

'Ergh argh und oorshlegargh!' she exclaimed before drifting out of frame.

Everyone was in hysterics, even Kristin.

'I'd drunk ten cocktails in half an hour,' she said.

'Well done,' said a fellow backpacker. 'You're a champion.'

By eight o'clock, the beer bongs had started. The beer bong is a length of plastic hose approximately 1.5 metres long and 5 centimetres in diameter. The protocol is as follows:

1) Fill the bong with beer. This involves a person at each end—the holder and the pourer. They should stand close enough together so the tubing makes a U-shape. The pourer tips a beer slowly into the tube until the bottle is empty. The night usually begins with stubbies, but progresses to long-necks (which fill the entire tube), and later mixed spirits.

2) The drinker holds one end, the tipper holds the other. The tipper is often elevated, standing on a chair or a table.

3) The drinker takes one end of the tube in his/her mouth, the tipper rapidly lifts his end into the air so the alcohol rushes down the tube into the drinker's throat.

4) If the drinker chugs the whole bong without stopping, gagging, asphyxiating or throwing up, he is given kudos, involving high-fives, backslaps, hugs and cheers. The faster he can chug it, the more he is appreciated and lauded.

Andy the Canadian didn't appear to be in possession of throat muscles. It was like pouring beer down a drain. He was considered a demi-god in the beer bong universe.

By some coincidence, the results of a study into the habits of British backpackers were published in the *Sydney Morning Herald* the following week. The good people at The National Drug and Alcohol Research Centre were proud to announce that after exhaustive research involving 1000 subjects interviewed in Sydney and Cairns, they could report that they drank like fish.

Officially 40 per cent reported drinking five or more days a week while in Australia, while only 20 per cent drank that much at home in the United Kingdom. The backpackers I met would call anyone who drank only five days a week a pansy. Anyone who drank less than five days a week would be a pansy wearing a skirt with pictures of pussycats on it.

In further shocking news, the study also found that these travellers were very fond of illicit drugs.

'The image of the hard-drinking, hard-playing UK backpacker appears to be reinforced by the results of this research,' said a study spokesman, whose name was possibly Dr S. Tate Bleeding-Obvious. Presumably he and his intrepid team are currently hard at work confirming that the world is, in fact, not flat.

The most praise one backpacker can have for another is this: 'They're all right, they really know how to party.' I heard variations on this sentiment every day. It's a point of honour among backpackers to drink a lot, to drink often, and to drink crap. Which brings us to goon.

Goon is also known as Chateau Cardboard, grape-based paint stripper and, more prosaically, cask wine. And like the Hills Hoist, Vegemite, and the Minogue sisters, it's an Australian invention. Perhaps predicting that in decades to come, his country would be overrun by backpacking hordes who needed to get as drunk as possible, as cheaply as possible, a guy called Tom Angove came up with the idea in the mid-1960s.

The chief advantage, and the initial reason behind the invention, was that it prevented oxidation. Once you open a bottle of wine, the air that enters the bottle starts to oxidise it. That's why if you don't drink a bottle of wine you've already opened within a few days, it goes off. The goon bag is designed so no air can enter it—the bag actually collapses as wine is poured out, so the wine can't go off from contact with the air.

Of course, the irony here is two-fold:

1) Most goon that backpackers buy is the cheapest available, so taste is not actually an issue.

2) Once it's opened it is consumed so quickly that the whole oxidation argument becomes immaterial.

South Australia in the mid-1960s was no doubt a quaint place where people actually opened a bottle of wine, had a glass or two, then recorked it for a couple of days until they felt the need to imbibe more alcohol. Thus there was a market for Tom Angove's ingenious invention. One wonders what he would make of his wine cask becoming the backpacker's buddy.

One also wonders what he would make of the curious practice of 'slapping the goonbag'—this is the ritual of removing the silver bag from the cardboard box and giving it a sharp whack before consuming. I could find no one who could explain this bizarre habit. A group of Irish girls did, however, refer to the bag as 'the silver pillow', explaining that after a big session with a gaggle of goons (a goongle perhaps?) the silver bags could be reinflated by blowing them up, and then, no matter where you happened to find yourself, you had a pillow on which to rest your throbbing head and sleep off the hangover.

Nearly every backpacker is aware of some very worrying entries on the list of ingredients for many cask wines. Included in these is the notice that the wine may contain egg, milk and fish products. (I later found out that egg whites, a milk protein, and a substance that comes from the inner membrane of the air bladder of the sturgeon are all used as agents to clarify wine, bonding with yeast, bacteria and tannins so these impurities can be removed.) But none of this seemed to bother the backpackers, even when they were informed that the type of wine they were consuming in such lethal amounts was usually the reserve of unfortunate guys who made their home on bits of cardboard laid out on city footpaths.

'It's cheap, and it does the job,' said Debbie, a 22-year-old Canadian who was the first person I asked about this, as we sat at the back of Indy's discussing the merits of alcohol that came in a cardboard box. 'Aren't all backpackers alcoholics, anyway?'

Her sentiments were echoed by every person I quizzed on the matter, along with some protests that the stuff was actually pretty good. Orlando Fruity Lexia; Stanley Classic Dry White; Sunnydale Medium White—they were all vintage according to my travelling companions. When it came to wine they never touched a drop that came from a bottle.

'See those stripes on the box?' said Killian, a 25-year-old from Dublin, patting his personal wine cask. 'Those are Ferrari stripes. This is top stuff. The *creme de la creme, je ne sais quoi.*'

Then he burped.

Industry figures show that cask wine represents around 70 per cent of wine sales by quantity in Australia. Surely among the backpacker community they're underestimating that figure by about 30 per cent.

*   *   *

Picnic is such a quaint word, don't you think? It brings to mind rugs and baskets and foods carefully prepared and sealed in various airtight containers. So when I heard that the hostel was organising a picnic for the next day in Bronte, a couple of kilometres south of Bondi, I wondered how exactly this was going to work. As it turned out, not much like a picnic at all.

The first thing we all had to do was put in ten dollars each. Volunteers were called on to help purchase supplies, and curious to see what would be bought, I put up my hand, along with four others. Led by hostel manager Megan, we went immediately to a bottle shop. The prices of slabs of a beer called Pure Blonde were ascertained. The money was counted and it was decided that four slabs would suffice. That's 96 bottles, and 20 people had put money in to the kitty. Food, the major consideration when organising any respectable picnic, was to be bought with the remainder, a paltry $25. Chips, cheezels and peanuts were purchased, and that was it.

Food is very low on the totem pole when it comes to the backpacker lifestyle. It's ranked just above hygiene. It is merely something which lines the stomach so that the backpacker can drink more. How it tastes or how good it is for you is of no consequence. Peruse the aisles of any convenience store in an area frequented by budget travellers and you will find an inordinate number of instant noodle options, from the 55 cent home brand variety to the 'deluxe' Maggi $2 packs. Add boiling water and you have something to momentarily satisfy your gullet, if not your gourmet sensibilities, in flavours that vaguely resemble everything from barbecue beef to chicken sweet and sour.

'Backpackers spend all their money on three things,' one convenience store owner in Bondi told me. 'Booze, condoms and 2-minute noodles.'

When we got to Bronte, a secluded grassy spot was found, well away from the children's playground. This was considerate because beers were immediately opened and spliffs rolled and lit. It was noon on a Tuesday. Welcome to the picnic. The drinking was steady for the next six hours, but that was nothing. It was just a bit of daytime lubrication, a warm-up for when the sun went down. And admittedly, it was interspersed with games of frisbee, cricket and volleyball.

After a particularly fierce game of frisbee, I got talking to Nick, a 23-year-old from Vancouver. He'd just finished a political science degree back home, was returning to university to study law, and worked two bar jobs simultaneously to save the money for this trip.

He was a hotshot during the frisbee game and it turned out there was a good reason for that. He came to Australia to compete in a global tournament called the World Ultimate Club Championship, which was held in Perth late last year. The game they play is a little like American football with a frisbee, so presumably just about nobody outside the sport understands it. Suffice to say, it's no walk in the park. Players end up running from 10 to 12 kilometres every game, and ankles and hamstrings tend to get sprained and strained because of overuse. But Nick claimed it was more than physical.

'You play with your mind as much as your body,' he said. '80 to 90 per cent of the game is mental. '

He was in the Canadian mixed team, which is called Team Fisher Price, and the men's team, called Furious George. Team Fisher Price won the mixed championships, but the Japanese dominated the rest of the competition, winning both the male and female tournaments. Nick informed me that the Australian team played the Japanese in the male final and acquitted themselves quite well. They're from Melbourne, and they're called Team Thong.

Nick talked a bit about his travels, and told me about a night out in Cairns, where he was standing at the bar attached to his hostel just talking to a friend, when out of nowhere, someone punched him in the face. He literally didn't know what, or who, had hit him.

'I think it's a game the locals play up there,' he said. 'The weird thing is the bouncers ended up throwing *me* out because I had blood all over my face.'

Wasn't he angry about this?

'Shit happens,' he said with a shrug. 'And because I was bleeding all these girls started paying attention to me, so that was okay.'

While we were talking, a Canadian girl walked up to squeals and hugs from some of the other backpackers. It turned out that she was staying at Indy's a few weeks ago and had hooked up with a local guy one night at a club in the city. She moved into his place in Manly.

'I'm so happy,' she told her friends. 'This morning he

made me fruit salad, he made me coffee, made me breakfast, then we had sex in the bath, and then he drove me here.'

They congratulated her on her good fortune, while I wondered whatever happened to that catchphrase 'too much information'.

The day passed in a blur of beer, smoke and sweat. There was talk of travel and of home, of the best places to stay up in Hervey Bay and Airlie Beach, and the progress of various football teams in the United Kingdom and Europe.

Jim, a 24-year-old from Glasgow, and Pat, a 23-year-old from Liverpool, were discussing work. Jim had been in Australia for a year, and he'd done three months of fruitpicking, which earns backpackers the right to apply for an extra one-year visa. He'd picked mangoes, sprayed weeds, and laboured on building sites.

'The work's okay, but surprisingly, the mango picking was the worst of the three,' he said. 'You get this itchy rash that can drive you insane. I earned $15 or $16 an hour on average. With labouring I got between $100 and $150 a day, cash in hand.'

Pat looked like a long-lost brother of Liam and Noel Gallagher. He had lank hair hanging from his Kangol cap, a cigarette constantly dangling from his mouth, and a laconic way of speaking. He'd also been here a year and during that time he bought a Toyota Hi-Ace van (the vehicle of choice among budget-conscious backpackers) and driven across the country.

'The van was stolen in Coogee two weeks ago,' he said. 'But you have to be philosophical about these things. It only cost me $400 anyway and it got me across Australia, so I'm not complaining.'

His story about losing his van, and the easy-come-easy-go attitude about his loss, echoed my old friend Kenneth's tale. Perhaps Australia really did have this effect on travellers. Or maybe our convict history just led them to expect the worst.

Pat had also been fruitpicking with a view to extending his time here, and he'd sprayed weeds at a mining site at Mt Keith, outside Kalgoorlie, for $19 an hour, working a 10-hour day with free bed and board. The day after the picnic he was going for his medical examination to get his second year visa, 'but I'm a bit worried because I haven't been looking after myself too well, if you know what I mean.'

In the late afternoon, with no picnic foods in evidence after the chips and peanuts disappeared in the first 15 minutes, I grabbed a bite to eat with a handful of backpackers who actually didn't mind shelling out for a sit-down meal at one of the local cafés. In the group was Tue, a permanently buoyant 27-year-old from Denmark, who spoke in a yodelly, lilting tone of voice. He was a scientist whose special area was protein chemistry.

'I want to visit every continent by the time I'm 40,' he told me. 'Now that I've been to Australia, the last two on my list are Africa and Antarctica. After that I want to go into space by the time I'm 50.'

Seriously?

'Seriously. I want to break free of the earth and everything on it for a while.'

Sitting next to him was Don, a 24-year-old from Ireland, who almost drowned yesterday. Seriously. He was six foot one and built like a rugby second-rower, but he didn't know what a rip was. He soon found out.

'I was out there talking away to my mate and then we realised we were being carried out to sea. I started swimming as hard as I could into the beach, but I was going backwards. I found out later this is the worst thing you can do.

My buddy said, 'Don't panic' and held onto me. He was able to get the next wave in but I couldn't catch it. I started yelling and waving to the surfers. Then the lifeguards came out along with all these cameras.'

The second season of the documentary TV series *Bondi Rescue* was being made, and the cameras followed Don as he was plucked from the water and then lectured on the sand about what to do should he ever be caught in a rip again. He was a little embarrassed, not only by the fact that his big moment of TV glory came from being half-drowned, but because he was saved by Brooke Cassell, the only female lifeguard on the beach.

The lifeguards at Bondi have a name for the notorious rip at the southern end of Bondi Beach.

'It's called Backpackers,' said Chris 'Chappo' Chapman, who was patrolling the beach the day before Don told me his story. 'That's because all the backpackers walk down from the hostels on Campbell Parade and Hall Street, or they get off the bus at the first stop when they get to Bondi, and go in the water right here.'

Locals used to call the rip the Bondi Tram or the Bronte Express because it could whip you out to sea and around to Bronte, two beaches away. Chappo estimated that 80 to 90 per cent of the people they save are tourists. Some don't speak English and can't read the warning signs, or the signs that tell them to swim between the flags. Others just don't realise how dangerous the surf can become. And others mistakenly think that where lifeguards are intently scanning the water is the safest place to be, when in fact the exact opposite is true—they're concentrating on the most notorious areas of the surf.

On a Saturday or Sunday in the middle of summer, there can be as many as 40,000 people on Bondi Beach. The lifeguards rescue around 2500 annually.

For Don's mother's sake, it was just as well the lifeguards were on the ball. After eating, we wandered back along the cliff walk that winds from Bronte to Bondi for two-and-a-half kilometres, and Don confessed he was on a bit of a mission while out here. In a couple of days time he'd be heading over to New Zealand to search for a long-lost brother who hadn't been heard from in two years.

'He left Ireland and then we just lost track of him,' he said. 'We know he was last heard of over in New Zealand, so I'm going to have to play detective and see if I have any luck. I know New Zealand isn't exactly a huge place, but I can't imagine it's going to be too easy.'

Little did that lifeguard know that when she dragged Don onto her board the day before, she might have been saving more than one person.

Don and I eventually caught up with the rest of the group at the last rocky outcrop overlooking Bondi Beach. Everyone had stopped to take photos. The sun was setting, the sky was bruising, and from the southern headland in the fading afternoon light of a summer's day, it really looked beautiful. Late surfers were catching the last waves of the day. The lights were starting to come on in the streets and apartments and houses, and they twinkled in the looming grey. The buildings jutted into the sky like sandcastles. You could hear the wind and the waves.

The grime, the noise, the sweat, the tackiness and the annoying, jostling humanity were so far below that they disappeared. It was like looking at Bondi as an alien would. And that alien would be very tempted to immediately disembark its spaceship and plunge into that paradise. But looks can be deceiving. He would last less than a week before scurrying back to whatever planet he called home, realising that some things are better off from a distance.

I have some news. I know how, where and when I'm going to die.

A skateboard is involved, but it is unclear whether I will be riding it or hit by whoever is riding it. It will be near the corner of Campbell Parade and Hall Street in Bondi. And apparently medical science is going to make giant leaps during my lifetime, because I will be either 135 or 155 years old.

This information was revealed to me by a man named Beautiful All. Yes, that really is his name. Okay, his given name was Barry McGrath, but 12 years ago he officially changed it. He showed me his passport, and sure enough, there it was—surname All, first name Beautiful.

'I looked in the mirror 12 years ago,' Beautiful said. 'And I said "Hey baby! There's only one name for you!"'

The man who told me this was 68 years old and looked like an extra from *The Lord Of The Rings*.

I'd heard about Beautiful from a friend who lived in Bondi. She told me that he often stood on the beach boardwalk with a bunch of handmade signs and informed everyone who walked past that they were beautiful, they were wonderful, and they were fully enlightened.

I tracked him down at Bondi Backpackers, a hostel on Campbell Parade, where he has rented a single room for the last three years. It's not hard to find his room. The door is covered with signs he's written, saying things such as 'You are fabulous', 'We have an absolutely perfect world' and 'Q: What does the world need today? A: Absolutely nothing.' These are interspersed with cut-out magazine pictures of horses, Gandhi and Janet Jackson. And right in the middle is a sign that reads:

Dear One,

What are your views? What if this old 'know-all' could learn something from a younger person? But would I really listen? Please try me! Please knock on the door!

So I did. There was no answer. The girl at the desk told me that he often went walkabout, so I slipped a note with my number under his door. A couple of days later I got a call.

'Is this Baz?'

Why do people immediately call me Baz, even if they hardly know me?

'Yes, I guess this is Baz.'

'I'm a Barry too, mate. But now I'm Beautiful.'

We organised to meet at his room in the hostel that afternoon. When I got through the door I was greeted by a skinny man with long wispy grey hair and a bald pate. He had silver-framed glasses, a grey beard and gleaming dentures. He wore a white singlet, loose harem pants and a headband. He had a flower behind one ear and a white spot painted on his forehead.

'Welcome to my home, Baz!' he exclaimed, handing me a tray which held a martini glass filled with water, a plastic container of pasta salad, a mango with 'BAZ' written on the skin in ballpoint pen, and a heart-shaped piece of coloured paper that bore the words 'You are beautiful'.

His room, which was roughly 4 metres by 4 metres, was wallpapered with his signs and pictures of girls in bikinis. Also in the room was a silent New Zealander with a shaved head, named Raj, who Beautiful introduced as his bodyguard and manager. Raj smiled a lot for a bodyguard and manager. He seemed like a nice bloke, although the most I heard him say over the next two hours was 'Nice to meet you'.

Beautiful, on the other hand, did not appear to be in possession of an 'off' switch. It took a while to get his story because he was very fond of a digression and a non-sequitur.

'Let's start,' he finally said after 20 minutes. 'I grew up in Grafton. I could knit you under the table, I could destroy you on a chessboard, and I could crochet you to death, Baz. John Wayne taught me all those things. He's on ice now, with Walt Disney, as you know. We went to see his house after he died and there was a big room full of dolls.'

I wasn't sure what this had to do with anything. Or if any of it made any sense. Or where it might have been going. But to keep the conversation rolling I mentioned that all the dolls may have had something to do with John Wayne's real name being Marion.

'Ah!' exclaimed Beautiful, as he pointed at me. 'That's right! A writer who does his research! We're going to get along fine, Baz!'

It was at that point he told me when, where and how I was going to die. I'd known him less than half an hour. The guy certainly had a way with timing.

Beautiful called himself a quarter-caste Aboriginal Jewish boy. His father, 'Darky' McGrath, was Aboriginal; his mother was white. He left school in Grafton at 17, then made the move to Melbourne, working in a bank in Collins

Street. But at night he indulged his passion for singing, performing in nightclubs in Prahran in the mid-1950s.

'I knocked them dead,' he claimed. 'I sang Johnny Mathis and Nat King Cole. But I was an exhibitionist and I wanted to conquer the world, so when I was 19 I went to America. I have a bigger ego than Slash and John Bon Jovi put together. In fact, my ego is bigger than the iceberg that sank the Titanic.'

Alas, his singing career was about as successful as the Titanic—the boat, not the movie. He ended up in Toronto in Bible college and then became a born-again preacher. His story from there was long, winding and a little fuzzy in places, but suffice to say, he married a Swedish woman, returned to Australia, and spent time in communes in Queensland and northern New South Wales. He alluded to time spent in jail in Coburg and Cairns for stealing and drugs offences. He smoked a lot of dope, but said he hadn't touched it in 14 years. He claimed that Keith Richards once came up to him and grabbed his arm to see what the tattoo on his shoulder said. It reads: I AM GOD'S SUPERIOR.

While living in Byron Bay from 2000 to 2003 he set up The Fairly Sirius Church Of The Occasional Giggle. It has 457 members, the patron saint is Billy Connolly, and the cost of membership is two used postage stamps.

What do they believe?

'We seriously believe with strong conviction that all religions come from God,' he said. 'At our commune in Byron I planted a whole lot of roses, and when they finally bloomed, they were all red. It was too much. I had to get in there and put in whites and yellows and all these other colours.'

He paused for a second, which is a long period of silence in one of Beautiful's stories.

'So too with our love of God, guys,' he said, looking from me to Raj and back again. 'You've got to have variety or it's ugly.'

Then Beautiful All gave me his four reasons for being here on earth. I'll now transcribe them verbatim for your edification.

1) To get attention. I love people looking at me.

2) I'm here to remind people of their glory. There's a guy who hates your guts, Baz. He's wearing a brown T-shirt with Santa Cruz written on the front of it. *(I'm actually wearing a brown T-shirt with Santa Cruz written on the front of it.)* We give ourselves the roughest time. Jesus, Krishna, Buddha, Mother Mary, Mother Teresa, Mohammed, Ghandi—they're all wonderful beyond words and let's elevate them all. But you and your grandmother are just as wonderful. Let's build a temple for Krishna. I admire the dude—he's on the head of my bed *(on a cushion cover)*. But let's build a temple for nanna. She's just as wonderful and glorious.

3) I'm really very, very interested in the Bible. I have seven translations here.

4) And I'm very interested in pornography.

He then took out some of his more recent signs, written in felt pen on big sheets of cardboard. He stood, flicked through them, reciting each card. The result was like a grizzled, crazy version of the famous film clip of Bob Dylan's 'Subterranean Homesick Blues'.

The signs said:

–Extra terrestrial life. I haven't seen a thing, but I'm a believer.

–Hey sexy. I'm so proud of you.

–Hey Spunky. You've got guts. You're an adventurer and you're fully enlightened already.

–Belittle yourself no more. You are really, really vast, sexy, glorious beyond words.

–Hey you! Yes you! Thanks for coming to our multiverse, darling. You are far above being majestic.

–Dear young people.

Out of sheer envy we hate you young people.

Q: Why?

A: Because of your wonderful hair, body, looks and sex life.

If you achieve fame and popularity in music and films, we're jealous.

Yours truly, oldies. (eg. your ego-tripping Guru Beautiful)

PS But deep down we know that you young people are fab beyond words.

Was Beautiful crazy? Did he do one too many trips in the 1960s? Was he just an old perve? Some locals said he was all three. But after a few hours I realised that my face was hurting because I'd been smiling so much.

I was almost out the door when he called me back.

'Baz, I forgot to say something else. I know you're on your way up and you're going to be a great writer...'

Here we go, I thought. He's flattering me because he's going to hit me up for money.

'...but I know it's only the start and it can be hard at the beginning. I don't have much, but if you find you're ever in need of anything, let me know, because I always have a few spare bucks. You know where to find me.'

The cynic in me felt a little ashamed, and a long way from enlightened. Sure, Beautiful All was an eccentric old bugger but he wasn't hurting anyone and his heart appeared to be more or less in the right place. As I crossed the road at the corner of Campbell Parade and Hall Street, I looked left and then right, checking for rogue skateboarders. I wasn't yet 135 years old but there was no point in taking chances.

It was one o'clock in the morning and I was standing in a bar in Sydney's CBD. Well, it was meant to be a bar. The floor was tiled, the smell was a combination of spilled beer and a faint trace of vomit, the ambience was truck stop-meets-RSL club.

This place had not been our first choice. Or second choice. Or third choice. It came at the end of one of those evenings where you spend most of your time walking between places, or standing in a queue waiting to get in somewhere, or sitting in a taxi trying to get to the queue to get in somewhere. And then the queue moves a metre in 20 minutes, so you decide to cut your losses and not wait another hour to get into the place, which advertises itself as a 'party bar' on Oxford Street in bustling, slightly seedy Darlinghurst, and totally caters to the backpacker market with drink deals, cheap meals, and theme nights.

So our group of eight walked to another bar closer to the city centre, where we were turned away by the bouncer because one of the girls we were with was wearing thongs.

'Well we don't want to come into your pissy place anyway!' yelled Brent, a wiry, wild-eyed Canadian who was way too intense for his own good. 'We were going to spend four hundred dollars in there! And now we'll take our money elsewhere! You're a loser!'

Brent led the way to another bar that he assured us would be a much better place for us to spend our money and our time. We followed him through Whitlam Square, the windblown crossroads between Hyde Park and Darlinghurst, and then down to a club that was attached to a backpacker hostel beautifully situated right in the middle of two of Sydney's busiest streets, opposite the city's biggest train station and a huge bus interchange. The bouncer asked to see our room keys. When we said we weren't staying at the hostel, he said we couldn't get in as it was a residents-only night.

'Well we don't want to come into your pissy place anyway!' yelled Brent, who certainly had this line down pat. 'We were going to spend four hundred dollars in there! And now we'll take our money elsewhere! You're a loser!'

Then Brent remembered another place he could take us.

'This place goes off!' he assured us, which made me wonder why he hadn't simply taken us there in the first place. 'We went there last Friday night and it was wall-to-wall babes. Swedish, Danish, German, French. It was like the United Nations of babedom in there.'

The United Nations of babedom was obviously in recess that night, possibly on a peace-finding mission in Ibiza, because there were roughly 50 people in the place, and 46 of them were men. And of the four women in the place, we had brought two of them with us. But at least we got in. I don't think I could have handled Brent's little speech again.

Dora wasted no time in shimmying up to random men and dancing suggestively in front them, then draping her arms around their necks. She was a friendly girl, although not exactly the most discriminating or cautious of women. Our other female companion, a petite Canadian called Tessa, seemed to have become attached to another member of our group, Chris from Melbourne.

'I've been hanging out with her for a couple of days now and put the hard word on her last night,' he told a couple of us while waiting to order some drinks and take them back to the table where they were sitting. 'I did all the groundwork but nothing happened. She didn't want to have sex in a room with seven other people in there.'

'Wow, that's just weird, isn't it?' I ventured, in a tone that was meant to convey sarcasm.

'I know,' he said, taking me seriously. 'I suggested we go

to the bathroom and do it in there. I mean, we were both drunk at the time. But she still said no.'

Meanwhile, the rest of the guys hovered at the bar, ordering jugs of beer and downing them as if they were middies. We were all just standing around shuffling our feet, and I got the distinct impression that everyone was thinking the same thing: 'This is really crap, but if we drink enough it mightn't seem so crap.'

I got talking to John, the older English guy with shaggy blond hair, who I'd met on that first afternoon on the verandah at Indy's. He first came to Australia on holiday five years ago, always wanted to return, and came back three months ago. He travelled up and down the east coast, then returned to Sydney. He'd been at Indy's for the last six weeks.

Six weeks? Didn't he find it a bit much after that long?

'It's easy to get stuck there,' he admitted. 'But that's not a bad thing. It's very easy to get attached to people very quickly. After two days you trust them with your passport, your wallet and your life.'

But what happened to backpacking being about adventure and experiencing new things and putting yourself outside your safety zone?

'Look, I know what you mean, but these days backpacking isn't about achieving anything. It's about the backpacker community. You're not working towards anything. I'm quite enjoying that at the moment and not beating myself up about it. I've been adventurous in the past but right now I'm happy hanging out.

'And as for everyone else, you've got to realise that they're 20, 21, 22, 23 years old, and Sydney is quite often their first stop when they come to Australia. It's quite an emotional upheaval to fly halfway around the world by yourself or with one other person. You get to Bondi and all of a sudden you've got the sun and the surf and all these other travellers just like you. It's a comfortable situation and it's hard to tear yourself away from that.'

But he wasn't in his twenties, was he?

'No, I'm 37. But backpacking keeps me young. The average age is probably 23 or 24. But I keep up. Some mornings I wake up and feel terrible, but I splash around in the sea, get some sunshine, have something to eat, and I feel better by eight o'clock that evening, and I'm ready to do it again.'

John was doing some shifts at Indy's reception, learning the ropes because he was going to be working there full-time in four weeks' time, and would eventually like to run his own hostel.

'You know what I like about backpacking?' he said to me. 'No matter how much money anybody has, no matter what walk of life they're from, or whether their family is upper class or lower class, when you're in a hostel you've got one bag with some clothes, an iPod, and whatever else you can fit in there. Everybody's the same here. It's quite a leveller.'

And then he went to the bar to buy another jug.

*   *   *

The next morning...well, the next morning probably happened, but none of us were up to see it. The next afternoon, I parked myself on the back verandah and for some reason, for the rest of the day, talk turned to sex.

'Bondi is the worst place in the world not to be getting action, man,' warned Gavin, a teacher from Cairns who was visiting Sydney on holidays. 'It's in your face all the time.'

And it really is. Girls flirt outrageously and guys strut around like peacocks. There are drunken fumblings in communal kitchens, on dance floors, in bunk beds and in toilets. It's not uncommon to wake up in the morning and look across to see two people in bed who you know just met that night. The backpacking trail is the biggest mobile pick-up joint on earth. The heat created by all this action should be visible from space.

I got talking about this earlier in my room with Dave the blonde Dutchman. Sex was an easy topic to bring up with him, as I'd just found a jumbo box of condoms lying on the floor and asked if they were his. Naturally, they were. He'd been staying in the hostel two weeks, and had had sex with five girls in that time.

'It's almost too easy,' he told me, blushing slightly. 'These English guys try to chat up the girls, but they get too drunk and then they can't do anything, so there's no competition.'

Andrew, a 23-year-old from Toronto had been at Indy's a month and had sex with six different girls.

'Everybody's looking over the new herd when they check in each morning,' he said. 'None of the guys here can deny it.

They're checking out who to latch on to. It's like a meat market with the cows parading in. Everyone here wants to gets laid, girls included.'

In fact, the inhabitants of Andrew's room had a code word when one of them brought someone back and they were about to indulge in some bunk action—'headphones'. It was an advance signal for everyone to don their personal stereo headsets if they wished to block out the carnal noises that were to follow.

'Hostels are by far the easiest places to pull,' he continued. 'And everything is no strings attached. Most of them I don't even know their last names. I almost feel bad about it, but at least I can remember their first names. Most of them anyway.'

Carrie was a 21-year-old Canadian and it would have been nice if Andrew remembered her name because she hooked up with him a few nights earlier. She had no illusions and agreed that casual sex was part of the package.

'I think anyone who travels like this realises that it's only going to be a fling. You have to be realistic. People are always moving on. It would have to be something crazy to turn into anything more. I wouldn't be against it but the chances of it happening are very slim.'

Mark, a New Zealander saddled with the very unimaginative nickname of 'Kiwi', told everyone he was 35 but admitted to me privately that he was actually 43. He said that even 35 was a little too old in backpacker circles because while he looked younger than his years, and he felt that the 'window of acceptability' with younger women was still open to him, the age difference made it more difficult than it used to be. Kiwi was a former photojournalist, who now worked on construction sites in remote mining sites for months at a time, then came to the city to stay in backpacker hostels and party for a while. He was remarkably frank about his intentions.

'My aim is to get laid,' he said, without blinking. 'I come in here and I'm surrounded by all these girls who are on holidays, out for a good time and sexed-up. And then I'm put in a room with them. What do you expect?

'Some of them are too young, though. If they're 18 or 19, I'm still attracted to them because they're hot, and they like me because I'm a friendly, outgoing guy, but they tend to just think of me as a friend, not as someone they'd want to have sex with.'

This was driven home to Kiwi one night when an Irish girl he had been getting along with famously looked into his eyes and said, 'I really like you, Kiwi. I wish I could hook you up with my mum.'

Chris and Dan were two 22-year-old buddies from Melbourne, who had driven up to Sydney for a holiday. Chris was the one who had failed to convince the Canadian girl to have sex with him in the dorm room or in the bathroom. A few nights ago, however, Dan and Chris were about to leave a club in the city when they noticed two Danish girls and started talking to them. The guys immediately invited them back to the hostel, saying they would drive them back home later.

'We got to the hostel, took them up to our room, and it was me and one girl in my bunk, Dan and the other girl in his bunk,' said Chris. 'When I woke up in the morning, I looked across and it looked like Dan was trying to chew his arm off to get away.'

'She was okay looking in the club,' said Dan. 'But the next morning I realised she didn't look too good. And she wouldn't say anything. She was weird. She wasn't the kind of girl I'd normally go for, but I'm on holidays so I'm going for anything.'

'So we said we were still drunk and couldn't drive them home,' said Chris. 'We showed them where to get the bus though.'

Were there other people in the room during all this?

'Yeah,' said Chris. 'But that happens all the time. Apart from us two, it was actually all girls staying in our room and we asked them beforehand if it was okay to bring girls back if we met anyone. They were cool, because they were already bringing guys back anyway.'

As I listened to all these stories of getting it on like rabbits, I thought back to when I did my first big backpacking stint in my twenties, trekking around the United Kingdom, Europe and the Middle East.

I'm sure my hormones were racing around in the same hyperactive state as my new travelling companions in 2007, but these tales they were spinning and these figures they were spouting made me sound like a monk. Was I looking back at myself through rose-coloured glasses? Somehow I remember being a lot more idealistic, a lot more naive, and a lot less capable of defining the line between lust and love, or between friendship and the potential for something more than friendship.

So please permit the page to go all wobbly for a second and for the sound of a rewinding tape recorder to spin through your head. My body is becoming less pale, my features more chiselled and less wrinkled, my teeth whiter, and—joy of joys—my hair is growing back. You're here. It's 1986.

I'd already hitch-hiked around England, Wales and Ireland, and when I got to the island of Arran off the coast of Scotland, there was Lorena sitting on the grass outside the youth hostel.

We exchanged the three questions that every young traveller exchanges when they meet someone for the first time. Where are you from? Where have you been? Where are you going? She was from Rome, she had been in London, and she was on her way to Edinburgh. I was from Sydney, I had been in Belfast, and I was going anywhere Lorena was going.

We spent the day riding bikes around the island and that night, trying to impress her, I made the worst spaghetti bolognese I have ever made in my life. Hey, you try finding good mince meat on an island off the coast of Scotland.

Anyway, she and her constant companion, a skinny girl called Marilena, left for Edinburgh the next day. I hit the mainland and stood on the side of the road, my thumb in the breeze, my heart in my mouth.

After four days of hitching across the country, I got to Edinburgh, and after being turned away from the overcrowded major youth hostel in town, finally found somewhere to sleep at an independently run place. As I was checking in, my two Italians wandered through the foyer. The *Twilight Zone* theme played through my head and we smiled at each other.

That night we went to a three-level party space with live bands, a nightclub, and a performance art area. Two out of three ain't bad. We went to the club and, somewhat incongruously, Morrissey played matchmaker. It was while we were dancing to The Smiths' 'Bigmouth Strikes Again', that Lorena started staring at me intently with a dreamy smile on her face. I later found out this was because she was short-sighted and she was embarrassed about wearing her glasses.

We weaved our way back to the hostel arm in arm, then crept downstairs to the dining room. There we sat on an old lounge and kissed for three hours. Finally, as we could barely keep our eyes open, we said goodnight at 4:30 a.m., and I stumbled my way up to a dark room full of bunk beds that was ringing with the sound of snores and reeking with the smell of old socks.

My Italian and I spent the next two days wandering the city, occasionally stopping in doorways or sitting on park benches to devour each other. It must have been truly revolting for passers-by but we didn't care. I distinctly remember the night the girls left for home as we saw the worst Goth band (is 'worst Goth band' an oxymoron?) on earth. Afterwards, I accompanied Marilena and Lorena to the station, had one long, last kiss and watched the tail-lights of their train fade into the dark.

We swapped addresses, just like you always did in those quaint days before mobile phones, email, myspace and Facebook. And I never thought we'd see each other again.

Soon I was back in London, and re-uniting with my old gang of friends as we all seemed to be travelling the world at that time. It was comfortable. It was fun. We could live there in a house in Hammersmith for months if we liked.

Within a week I had booked a ticket for Rome.

The moment I arrived, I went to find Lorena. That night we were wandering the piazzas and winding streets, doing exactly the same thing we did in Edinburgh.

Strangely, sex didn't enter the equation. Well, okay, the thought entered my head roughly once every 60 seconds. But Lorena lived with her parents. And although her grasp of English was slim, I got the feeling that she was happy to carry on this strange alfresco affair, breezing through parks, leaning against statues, or sharing long puppy dog stares in crowded restaurants.

I left a week later. Travel time isn't the same as real time. It's elastic. You multiply everything by four or five. It was time to move on. Three weeks after that, while in Turkey, I met a German girl called Charlotte, and fell head over heels.

She had a boyfriend called Hans back at home, but she was also having an affair with a guy called Fredrick, a complicated situation which she would recount to me in limited English over long dinners and sightseeing, as I slowly cracked and crumbled inside.

I followed her all the way to Munich and ended up sleeping in a sleeping bag on the floor of her tiny university apartment room. When she got up early for lectures, she would gently wake me up, offer me her warm bed, and then leave for the day. In the mornings I'd walk around the city, buy groceries, and when she returned in the late afternoon we'd go jogging together in the old Olympic village. While we made dinner we'd listen to Tom Waits. Then I'd go out to bars with Charlotte and Hans one night, Charlotte and Fredrick the next.

It was pure torture but kind of delicious, too. I was suffering for unrequited love. How very noble. My nobility lasted two weeks.

You might find it strange that I look back so fondly on these two experiences, as neither of them ended in the wild exchange of bodily fluids. In fact, with Charlotte we didn't even get to the kissing phase.

But that's not the point. I was nowhere near home. I was in love with the idea of love and romance and travel and strange places, and girls who barely spoke my language. I was a world away.

A year after I returned to Australia, Charlotte visited Sydney with Hans, who was now her fiancé (Fredrick was never mentioned again). They stayed a night with me. Early the next morning Charlotte and I went down to the beach together. She challenged me to a swimming race, out to a moored boat and back. She won. As we were sitting on the sand getting our breath back, she started chuckling to herself.

'What's so funny?' I asked.

'Remember when you turned up at my door in Munich?' she said. 'I thought you were a crazy man.'

Maybe I was. Sometimes I wonder what happened to that guy.

Looking back over my diary of that trip from two decades ago, I'm stunned by the number of girls I met, hung out with and totally failed to have sex with.

In White Park Bay on the coast of Northern Ireland, I went out drinking and then for a long moonlit walk with a beautiful 19-year-old Israeli girl who was heading home in two days' time to do her national military service, and absolutely nothing happened.

On the Greek island of Santorini I went moped riding, swimming and even shared a room for a few nights with a sexy Swiss girl who was seven years older than me, and absolutely nothing happened.

And according to what I've got in front of me here in a weathered blue notebook, on 22 September 1986, I spent the whole day and night with Marion—we met up at Waterloo station, went to Tower Bridge, walked around the docks, had lunch on an old clipper ship, strolled for ages through Regent's Park, dozed in the sun on the grass for a while, drank and had dinner at the Globe Tavern in Baker Street, and ended up having a late night wander and coffee in Piccadilly.

This all sounds very idyllic and quite promising, but as I'm reading this diary for the first time in 20 years, I realise something—I can hardly recall who the hell Marion was. If I rack my brain, I seem to remember she was Austrian, but I have no idea where or when I met her. My diary mentions that we walked the streets arm in arm, she fell asleep in the park with her head on my shoulder, and I was somewhat tortured about whether I should make a move and try to kiss her at some point, but not only can I not remember what she looked like, I'd completely forgotten she even existed, until now.

However, there is one thing I'm sure about. Absolutely nothing happened.

Andy wasn't in his element being on dry land. I'd noticed him for a couple of days, quietly reading in the sun at the back of the hostel, silently listening to conversations, and joining in with the drinking when it suited him. He spoke softly, and not very often. He had a half-smile constantly on his face, which was stubbled, suntanned and lined, and framed by long, sun-bleached hair.

Andy wasn't your regular backpacker. He was 34 years old and was born in Houston, Texas, but for the last eight years he'd lived on a boat off Honduras and worked as a skipper on charter boats.

'Life's a game,' he quietly told me after we'd been talking for a while. You had to lean in to hear him speak. 'I've met people who have no money who are at the bottom of the game, and they're not happy. I've met really rich people who are at the top of the game, and they're not happy. So I got out of the game.'

He hadn't planned on being in Australia, and he certainly hadn't planned on being on terra firma for quite so long, either. He was wandering around a marina in Panama and noticed a 38-foot catamaran with a for sale sign on it. He was curious and got talking to the guy on board. It turned out the boat had just been sold but he had to get it to Australia. Five days later, Andy was on board and on his way here.

It took 79 days to get from Panama to Brisbane and the trip started with three people. It ended with two. The skipper and his girlfriend broke up on the way, and she jumped ship in the Marquesas Islands in French Polynesia.

After getting to Brisbane, Andy took off again and spent a month in Thailand, then came back to Australia in early December, just over a month ago.

'This is the longest I've been on dry land for years,' he said. 'It still feels a little strange.'

I wondered if Andy didn't also feel a little strange in this environment, among people in their twenties who just wanted to party all the time.

'They're young,' he said. 'They don't have much life experience. They want to party. That's fine. I understand what they're doing. With the way the world is at the moment, why not? Maybe it's the only response.

'There's a lot of blah blah blah around here. You're not going to hear much philosophising. I enjoy partying every now and then, but I like going somewhere where the music's not so loud so you can actually hear someone's conversation and maybe learn something from them. You have to get out there in the woods or the outback to hear people who have something to say.'

He'd finish saying something, then just sit quietly, smiling to himself, waiting to hear if I wanted to ask anything else. I felt a bit like Luke Skywalker quizzing Yoda. Then he told me something about the 79 days he spent trying to get here.

'On a regular boat, you get used to the rhythm of the boat making its way through the water, even in big seas. Your body eventually gets in synch with the boat.

'But with the catamaran you've got the two hulls, so it's like, BANG...bang-bang-bang...BANG-BANG...bang-BANG...BANG-bang-BANG...bang-BANG-bang-BANG-BANG. Your body's rhythms don't adjust to it, so it's difficult. You never really get used to it.'

I hadn't spent two-and-a-half months getting here, but I knew exactly what he meant. I was only a week into this adventure, and although I'd faced no treacherous seas, I already felt out of whack with my surroundings and my own internal rhythm.

I said goodbye to Andy, shouldered my backpack and headed to the bus stop. It was time to head north. My heart went bang-BANG-BANG-bang-BANG.

PART 2

BYRON BAY

Why have I brought my entire toy collection with me on the bus to Byron Bay? There are my tin lunchboxes featuring The Partridge Family and the Six Million Dollar Man, there's my Batmobile and car from The Man From UNCLE, there's a stack of boardgames, and there are my 1500 breakfast cereal toys, among other things. Apart from making me look like a 40-year-old virgin, it's going to take me an hour to pack everything up because I have it all strewn around my seat.

The bus driver won't be happy. He hasn't been happy the whole trip. He gets on the microphone and warns us to keep our legs out of the aisle. He constantly tells us not to bring hot food, unopened drinks or milk-related products onto the bus. He rouses us from fitful slumber every two-and-a-half hours to get off the bus for a compulsory break. And that's exactly what we're doing now.

I disembark and keep half an eye on the bus to make sure no one steals any of my collection. But I'm starving so I go into the roadhouse to eat. I can't remember what it is I order, but it tastes suspiciously great considering the usual fare at these places is coagulated, deep fried, limp, or a combination of all three. And there seem to be staff everywhere, fussing about the customers and whisking in and out of the kitchen. This is a pleasant change. I finish and move to leave when I'm approached by three waiters.

'Excuse me, sir,' says the first.

'There's been a mistake,' says the second.

'You were served the wrong meal,' says the third.

'It's okay,' I tell them. 'I really liked what I got.'

But they're not happy with this situation. One of them is consulting a clipboard and furrowing his brow. Then another folds up a serviette and presses it to my stomach. He pulls it away and I see it's stained with what's meant to be blood, but is pretty obviously tomato sauce that they put on the serviette beforehand. Then another starts pulling a linen tablecloth out of his mouth. Just when I think I've walked into a diner run by David Lynch, everyone freezes as they listen to a deafening voice.

'Folks, we're just coming in to Macksville for our next meal break.'

And I wake up from my dream.

Although I have never been subjected to torture in an eastern bloc country, I imagine it would involve some variation on a long-haul overnight bus trip in Australia. Catching the Greyhound—or 'riding the dog'—not only takes a lot longer than flying, it takes a lot longer than driving. In fact, it's only marginally more efficient than walking.

Every few hours the bus will stop, the driver will wake everyone up, then you have to get off the bus and wander around for half an hour in a dazed state in an over-lit service station in the middle of nowhere. Some people choose to make this situation worse by ordering food, chomping on limp hamburgers at odd times like 4:30 a.m., while sitting in orange moulded plastic seats and blinking like recently surfaced mole rats in fluorescent lighting so bright that after 20 minutes you walk out with a tan.

Meanwhile, the not-quite-tuned-in radio that is playing the worst of the 1960s, 1970s and 1980s is regularly interrupted by a lank-haired, unsmiling woman who coughs into the food and then yells out, 'Number 36! Fish and chips!' Which is scary for many reasons, the major one being that someone has ordered fish in a place that is not only nowhere near water, but nowhere near anywhere.

Intrigued, I peeked at this particular meal when it went past me and observed that the fish was shaped like a perfect isosceles triangle. I wondered what particular sea creature was shaped like a perfect isosceles triangle, and despite the fact that I'm not a qualified marine biologist, I came to the conclusion that there were none.

I walked outside for a while, and then sat on a grassy verge behind the petrol pumps, the intoxicating aroma of diesel and cigarettes mingling somewhat dangerously in the air. Macksville is kind of in the middle of nowhere, but we weren't really in Macksville. We were in a roadhouse on the edge of Macksville, which meant we weren't kind of in the middle of nowhere. We were exactly in the middle of nowhere.

Two other passengers joined me in the pre-dawn darkness, the soundtrack provided by a chorus of crickets and the occasional electronic fizz and pop of a glowing blue insect zapper. The overall effect was like an instrumental on a Nine Inch Nails album.

The Dutch guy had been staying in Manly while in Sydney. His friend was Australian, and lived in Newcastle.

'I didn't like the salt water in the Manly surf,' the Dutch guy told me. 'It stung my eyes. And I think the hostels are very expensive.'

Yes, I thought. And Holland is too flat, and the food tastes like it was made in a prison, and no great pop music has ever come from there, and you're making me wish an English person would come along right now so I could discuss the deficiencies of Australian beer with him.

His Australian friend was taking his buddy up to Coffs Harbour and then to Queensland, to 'show him the real Australia'.

Aussie: We're going to Surfers because it goes off. And I'm showing him Dreamworld and Wet 'n' Wild. Lots of rides.

Dutch guy: *(Suggestively)* Ah, you like the rides, yes? But I think it's not those rides you like best. Other rides, yes?

Aussie: Yeah, man. Other rides. *(To me)* My girlfriend's not with me on this holiday, if you know what I mean.

Dutch guy: What goes on the road stays on the road.

As we got back on the bus, the Australian asked me, apropos of nothing, if I'd ever been to Woolgoolga on the north coast of New South Wales. I told him I hadn't.

'Good,' he says. 'Don't go there.'

Why's that?

'Full of Indians. They own the place.'

Indeed, the Sikhs make up a large proportion of Woolgoolga's population. They also happen to have been there building a strong community since the turn of the twentieth century, some time before this little Australian bigot entered the world to share his views.

Australia is a land of big things. There are big oceans all around it, and a big expanse of outback covering a lot of it, and a big rock in the middle of it.

But Australia is also a land of Big Things. These are large icons that have been built along the highways and byways of this great land, which elicit cries of, 'Oh God, that's so kitsch, keep driving!' or 'Oh God, that's so kitsch, stop the car so we can take photos and buy souvenirs!'

At last count, there were almost 150 of these Big Things scattered around the country. Usually the Big Thing will represent an animal or fruit or vegetable that is associated with the area.

For instance, the bus has passed the Big Banana in Coffs Harbour. When I was a kid on a road trip with my parents and brother and sister on the way to Surfers Paradise, this was an essential stop along the way. We would walk inside the Big Banana (yes, you could actually walk inside the Big Banana!) and pretend to be interested in the displays that explained everything about the growing and harvesting of bananas. But really we were just waiting to get through to the end, so we could go to the attached shop and buy a chocolate-covered banana on a stick, or a big frosty banana milkshake.

Back then the Big Banana really did seem big. Of course, like visiting your old primary school playground as an adult, it's a lot smaller than you remember it. And as I looked out of the bus window, I felt a little melancholy for two reasons—one, it did look quite small and sad, and two, not one other person in the bus noticed it apart from me. We glided by, and it was gone in 20 seconds, unheralded, unnoted, unphotographed, unloved.

Admittedly, a banana as long as a backyard swimming pool, fashioned out of concrete and fibreglass, isn't really something to write home about. Let's face it, a banana isn't that interesting, or even much of a stretch for a sculptor of kitsch big things, even if it does have it all over even less interesting oversized sculptural tributes to foodstuffs such as The Big Macadamia Nut in Nambour, Queensland, or The Big Potato in Robertson, New South Wales, of which many a child on a long, boring car trip has noted cruelly, but quite accurately, that it looks like The Big Turd.

Still, Australia takes its Big Things seriously. So seriously that a couple of months after my return from this trip, *The*

Sydney Morning Herald actually reported on the return of The Big Merino. Admittedly, it wasn't a very big story, and it was on page 13, but still, we are talking about a 15-metre tall sheep made out of cement and fibreglass, which on the whole, with the war in Iraq, the drought at home, and any other number of big, historic or catastrophic things going on right now in the world, isn't something you expect to read about in a quality broadsheet.

The locals had nicknamed the sheep Rambo, presumably because he was a ram, and he was big, dumb and had trouble speaking, just like Sylvester Stallone. Since 1985, Rambo had stood on a busy section of highway outside Goulburn in the New South Wales southern highlands. You walked in at hoof level, and after making your way through the gift shop on the ground floor, and an exhibition about the wool industry on the second floor, you could climb up into his head and gaze across the landscape through the plate glass windows of his eyes.

As a kid, I always thought it would have made an excellent lair for an evil genius who planned to take over the world. Or take over Goulburn anyway. But if he was planning on taking over Goulburn, he couldn't have been much of an evil genius. Just an evil idiot.

Alas, in 1992, the highway was re-routed, so Rambo became a very lonely sheep on a stretch of road that few used anymore. The 2007 newspaper report trumpeted the announcement that some local businessmen were going to cut Rambo free, lift all 96 tonnes of him onto a truck and transport him just under a kilometre away to a service station on the highway. Once again the oversized ovine would gaze mutely over a line of cars, and a new generation of children would pester their parents to stop so they could wander around inside a giant farm animal.

As the bus whizzed past banana plantation after banana plantation, I wondered if the Big Banana would have inspired as much media attention as the Big Merino if it had found itself in the same situation, and the highway had been diverted around Coffs Harbour. Could a lonely banana arouse the same pathos as a lonely sheep? Which was more iconic? Surely it would be more difficult to muster sympathy for a piece of fruit than a woolly animal.

It was at this point I began to wonder if I may have been on this bus a little too long.

Soon afterwards the Australian guy who I'd met at the Macksville roadhouse started waving at me from his seat a few rows down the bus. I waved back half-heartedly and then he pointed frantically towards the window out the right-hand side of the bus. I looked, and there on a hill in the distance was another big thing. A white temple. We were passing Woolgoolga. I looked back at him and he scrunched up his face and shook his head in a look of distaste. I smiled weakly at him. I had definitely been on this bus too long.

Three hours later, after passing through Grafton (claim to fame—home of wide streets and jacaranda trees!) and Maclean (claim to fame—Australia's most Scottish town!) our driver announced that we were approaching our last rest stop before Byron Bay. But we were merely a half hour away from our final destination.

'Keep driving, man!' I yelled. 'End this misery! Come on everybody! Who's with me? Let's vote! Who wants to end this senseless waste of time stopping at some godforsaken service station, and keep driving instead?'

But of course I didn't yell that. I just sat there in a half-awake state, surrounded by the smell of body odour and farts, and silently waited for another delay in the middle of nowhere.

'We'll be departing after this meal-stop at 9:55,' our driver said over his microphone. 'And by 9:55, I mean 9:55. If you get back here at 9:56, you'll be seeing the back of the bus disappearing down the highway. Okay? We're leaving Ballina at five to ten.'

Ballina.

Ballina?

Ballina!

It couldn't be, could it? In the back of my mind I recalled a service station in Ballina that featured a Big Thing. Sure enough, we pulled up and there it was. The Big Prawn.

I got out, I walked around it, I took photos, and I bought a souvenir keyring with my name embossed on it. It was tacky. It was kitsch. It was ridiculous. But I had been on a bus for 12 hours and a large crustacean astride a petrol station provided a worthy diversion. And it was much, much cooler than The Big Macadamia Nut.

As I'm such a well organised traveller, I'd left accommodation inquiries to the night before I got to Byron, phoning around from Bondi with an increasing sense of desperation. After the receptionists at various backpacker hostels had calmed down from laughing at me, they gleefully informed me that there wasn't a bunk bed to be had in the whole town.

I end up finding a place in Belongil, a 20-minute walk from the centre of Byron, further up the beach. The area used to be called Struggle Town because it was the site of the major reason for Byron's existence—the meatworks. It was a working man's town back in the 1970s, and this is where the men and their families who relied on the abattoir came to live. By all accounts, the smell was terrible. The meatworks closed down in 1983 and Byron Bay became a place without a purpose. That's when the council decided that the major industry would shift from meat to tourism. A house in Belongil recently sold for $8 million. It smelled a lot sweeter in Belongil these days, if you could afford to live there.

By some strange coincidence I was staying at exactly the same spot I stayed the only other time I had ever been to Byron back in 1992. I'd been up to Brisbane to cover a music festival for a magazine, and along with my then girlfriend, I'd driven down the coast to hang out for a few days. It was idyllic. We didn't do much of anything apart from swim, walk, read and eat.

But even back then I remember people talking about how Byron wasn't the same place it used to be. They complained that it had lost its small-town feel and hippy roots. They spoke darkly about evil developers. But it still seemed pretty laidback to the two of us. Once you'd spent one night in town, you'd exhausted the nocturnal entertainment options.

I wondered how much it might have changed in 15 years. Would people today talk about 15 years ago as the best time to have been in Byron? Maybe everyone thinks that 15 years ago from any point in time was when things were best in the world.

I booked in and found my room, which was one of many set around a wooden U-shaped balcony that looked over a lush garden. It had the feel of a 1970s beach house. I opened the door and a figure in the bottom bunk on the far side of the room groaned and shielded its eyes from the sun. It then rolled over to face the wall and was still. I found out later it was English, it had a massive hangover, and it went by the name of Stuart, but at that point none of this information was forthcoming.

I found an empty bed, dumped my stuff, and as I was hot and tired, immediately crossed the road and dived into the ocean. It was a searing afternoon, and after unsuccessfully trying to catch a few of the weak, choppy waves, I just lay in the water for half an hour, feeling it cool my bones. The crowds were all down the town end of the beach, but up here there were just a few people scattered on the sand, and I was one of only half a dozen in the surf.

I sat on the beach for a while and gazed at one thing in Byron which I knew for a fact hadn't changed since I was last here. The Wreck, as it's known, is the half-submerged remains of the *Wollongbar*, a boat that lies around 30 metres offshore. It was here back in 1992, and in fact it's been there for over 70 years, since it broke free from the old pier during a cyclone and sank.

Then I walked along the beach and into town to meet up with my friend Paul. A New Zealander who lived in Bondi for 20 years, he made the seachange to Byron two-and-a-half years ago. Paul's an artist who has worked for Mambo and designed surfboards, T-shirts, album covers and band posters, and in 2006 we collaborated on a kids' book about heavy metal. He said he was moving to Byron to concentrate on his work, but I thought exactly the opposite might happen. I'd heard of people moving here and getting lost. The slowed-down pace and the holiday atmosphere meant that while they came here to get inspired and to focus their energies, instead their minds wandered and they flaked out. For Paul, that didn't happen, and he was busier now than when he was in Sydney.

We'd organised to meet at the Beach Hotel, which was famously owned by John Cornell, who was Paul Hogan's business partner when the two had huge success with *Crocodile Dundee*. It was built in 1990, and the day it opened for business is generally regarded as the turning point in Byron's direction towards becoming a more upmarket tourist destination. It's a sprawling place right across from the beach, with a big beer garden and a succession of large bars.

I found Paul sitting at a table sketching on the back of a drinks coaster with a felt tip pen. He pointed out Michael Hutchence's brother Rhett a few tables over, and a local character named Frenchie, who goes from pub to pub, maniacally darting around, checking out women and saying hello to random people, some of whom he actually knows.

Paul was the first of a few locals I spoke to who said that Byron hadn't really changed too much over the years.

'I've been coming here for 20 years, and it's really not a lot different,' he said, after I came back from the bar with a couple of beers. 'Yeah, there are more people, so it's more crowded than it used to be, but there's still just one main street, and the same three pubs where everyone still goes to drink. The Rails *(the Railway Friendly Bar)* is exactly the same as it was ten years ago. Some of the same bands are still playing there.'

Although Paul had found it to be exactly the place he needed to be creative and also indulge his love of surfing, he admitted that many who move here do drift off into a hippy haze.

'People tend to just shut off. They say things like, 'I haven't watched TV in a couple of months' like it's a really great achievement. I'll go into a café at two o'clock in the afternoon, and the *Sydney Morning Herald* will be sitting there untouched.

'They don't want to know what's happening in the world. They're ultra-aware of things that go on here, like overturned garbage bins in Jonson Street. They can all talk about their Pilates and shiatsu massages, but they don't know anything about the big issues of the world and they don't get popular culture references at all.'

He took a sip of his beer.

'You know what life here is like? It's like when you've been on the dole for too long, and you think, 'Man, I've got to post that letter tomorrow.' Tomorrow comes, and it gets to the end of the day, and you realise you didn't get around to it. Life really does slow down to that level for a lot of people here.'

After dinner, Paul dropped me back at the hostel, and I heard a guitar being played as I rounded the corner to get to my room. I was about to meet a muscled, tattooed affirmation machine.

Steve was 24 years old and he was on the run. Not from the law, but from himself. He said that he had been living in Ingleburn in Sydney's western suburbs for a year, but 'there was a lot of bad energy for me there'.

I heard a lot of people talk about energy—good or bad— while I was in Byron, but coming from the mouth of a guy who looked like Henry Rollins was a new twist.

'I packed my bag and my guitar last week and came here,' he said. 'I'm moving on.'

I know that sounds like a cliché, as if I'm making it up. But that's exactly how he spoke. Steve was intense and New Age at exactly the same time. It was a slightly unnerving combination. He spouted aphorisms that sounded like they'd come directly from a self-help book. But he spoke in a quiet, level tone that made you aware he sincerely believed what he was saying.

He produced two crystals from his pocket, and told me that one was to attract good things and the other was to repel bad things. He then brought out a silver disc with a swirled pattern engraved on it, and said that it was passed on to him 'by someone very important to me, who knew I needed it at the time. I'm only keeping it as long as I need it, and then I'm passing it on too. That's how it works'.

I couldn't laugh for a few reasons. Firstly, he wouldn't get the joke. Secondly, if it worked for him to think this way, then why not just leave him to it? And thirdly, he could have snapped me like a twig should his newly found peace and love vibe have suddenly lifted.

I asked what he did for a living and he talked about doing bar work back in Sydney, and alluded to something else without going into details. The way he mentioned it and then passed over it suggested that it was something either embarrassing, shady or illegal. I assumed it was drug dealing.

A couple of hours later it emerged that he was a stripper. But, of course, he wasn't like all the other strippers.

'I was giving a performance and I was giving of myself. The other guys were just showing off and they didn't even like these women. I wanted to give a piece of myself to them and put on the best show I possibly could.'

Steve was a very intense young man with a self-belief that was stunning for an ex-stripper who was hanging around a backpackers hostel in Byron.

A German girl named Jenny walked in. Steve already knew her so she sat down and started talking about her day, how she went from shop to shop in Byron, looking for work. She looked exhausted. Steve encouraged her to keep trying and then gave her a pep talk. He did this by espousing his own merits.

'I know I have so many skills,' he told her, then looked at me and fixed me with an unblinking gaze, before turning back to Jenny again. 'I have a lot to offer. I can do anything. I could walk into any bar, tell the manager that I'll work that night for free and by the end of the night, I'm so good that he'll hire me. I can pick up music by ear. I can teach both of you how to surf in one afternoon. I can teach people how to train. I can teach people how to eat properly.'

'How do you eat properly?' Jenny asked.

'You need good food,' he said, holding out his upturned left palm, and staring at her intensely.

'And you need good attitude,' he added, holding out his upturned right palm. Then he brought his hands together.

Jenny, to her credit, suddenly looked like she was about to fall asleep. Steve took this as his cue to sing a song that he'd recently written about his spiritual journey. Waves, birds, clouds and his soul were mentioned in the lyrics. I nodded in appreciation at the end when he looked up for a reaction, hoping that the curious mixture of embarrassment and terror I was feeling was not showing on my face.

I felt like a heel the next morning. The night before, Steve had asked if I played guitar.

'I do, but pretty badly,' I'd said.

He'd handed it over and I played a few things, and he'd nodded and smiled, and even asked about the fingering on one fiddly bit that looked complicated but was, in fact, pretty simple.

As we were sitting outside our room trying to wake up in the morning sun, he said, 'Any time you want to borrow my guitar to have a play, just come in and grab it. I mean, anytime. What's mine is yours.'

He was all right. He was 24 and his life had taken a bad turn and he was asking questions and searching for something. My default mode is cynic/sceptic. It's just that flaky new-age talk always makes me want to grab people by the throat and gently shake them, or maybe slap them around the head until reality slowly dawns on them and they stop speaking like woolly-headed throwbacks.

But one should know the enemy. So I decided to spend 24 hours seeking out the flaky and the woolly-headed, to fight my natural instinct to avoid or maim them, and to actually listen to what they had to say.

After a morning swim and some breakfast, I walked down the beach and into town, my new-age radar on full alert. Along Jonson Street, which is Byron's main drag, I saw a community noticeboard and stopped to have a look at some of the flyers. But what I read did not turn me into a sensitive new-age guy. It just fuelled the cynic within. Allow me to tell you about three of them.

The Path Of Love was described as 'a journey so deep, so terrifying, so joyous...so loved and supported...a journey home'. I imagined these words being intoned in a deep, rumbling manner much like the voiceovers used to promote Hollywood blockbuster films. James Earl Jones, who provided the voice of Darth Vader, and was a much-favoured movie narrator, would be perfect for selling The Path Of Love. The flyer went on: 'The Path Of Love is an intensive, highly structured seven day process in which participant's (sic) are supported to passionately focus on their sincere desire or longing to realise their full human and spiritual potential.' By the sound of things, a by-product of this would be the ability to describe something in a string of namby-pamby words that filled up a lot of space and said absolutely nothing.

The second one I read was simply called Earthing. 'We have lost our connection with the earth,' it read, opening with uncharacteristic bluntness. 'Pollution, global warming, and vanishing wildlife are all indicaters (sic) of how man has lost touch with the planet.' But how to reconnect with dear old Mother Earth? Fortunately the good people of Earthing had the answer—an earthing weekend. A group of 'up to 15' would be taken out into bushland to camp overnight. After a talk around the campfire from Dr David Saxon (it didn't specify what kind of doctor David Saxon actually was), each participant would take their swag (provided by the Earthing folk) to a patch of ground that they felt a 'kinship' with. They would camp there for the night. 'The next morning, each person will relate their experience to the group. Previous participants have been amazed and delighted at the insites (sic) that have been given to them.' Each person takes home a small pot of soil taken from the site where they slept, in which they are to plant a small shrub. 'As you watch the growth of your plant, reflect on the growth that you are making as a result of earthing yourself.'

Finally, there was Yummy. Yes, Yummy. You'll be excited to know that it's an acronym, and it stands for Yoga of the Universal Mother Matrix of Yamala. It is run by a woman called Lelema Sjamar, who gets kudos from a Hawaiian Ascension teacher, channel and artist, really the kind of guy you'd like a reference from when trying to impress someone. Lelema had a similar case of verbal diarrhoea when it came to describing what she had to offer: 'From the heart of Yamala we offer you a Pathway to activate the flow of universal love within sound movement interconnection manramudra.' Which, of course, all makes perfect sense, if you happen to come from Venus. *(Okay, I have a confession to make. Of the three new-age flyers I describe from the bulletin board, two are the real thing and one I completely made up. Can you guess which one is the fake? Turn to page 150 for the answer.)*

I kept walking, and in the next block I saw big posters for not one, but two performers who dabble in what I'll call the 'flaky arts'. There was a huge hoarding above the Great Northern Hotel for Shane St James, who was described as 'the most happening hypnotist in the world today'. As a slogan, it ranked just a little ahead of 'Reg, the hippest stamp collector in Pymble last Tuesday'.

Less than 60 seconds later, I saw a poster for The Space Cowboy. Unlike the character with the same name in Steve Miller's song from 1973, he was apparently not a joker, a smoker or a midnight toker, but a skinny dude with multiple facial piercings, holding up a bunch of bent cutlery. Space—if I may be so bold as to call Mr Cowboy by his first name— was billed as a World Champion Thought Reader. This took me by surprise, as up to this point I had been completely unaware of the fact that they held world championships in thought reading. But then I realised it made sense. They wouldn't bother announcing when or where the championships were being held, as anyone that was eligible to enter would be able to read the organisers' minds and just turn up to compete.

I eventually got to the end of the main street. This took roughly four-and-a-half minutes. Then I started wandering back on the side streets and saw places advertising beading workshops, art classes, holistic healing, and 'beadz and hair wrapz'. Using the letter 's' to signify a plural was obviously considered way too square.

And then I came across something called a wellness centre. On the sign outside it listed the different practitioners and their specialties. Ashiya did intuitive card readings, spiritual guidance, and aura and chakra clearing. Jade Rose did something called Hawaiian bodywork, which apparently involved 'relaxation and healing for your body, mind and spirit'. And Debra's deal was 'goddess readings, relaxing massage and the art of the sacred touch'. Was it just me or did Debra's skills sound suspiciously like they'd be better utilised in an establishment with a red light glowing outside the front door?

As I was curious, I wandered through the front yard and into the open door. It was very pleasant, a freestanding house with a wide verandah, tucked away in a quiet street in a quiet town, which as you can imagine, was very quiet.

I hung around in the hallway/reception area, but there didn't appear to be anyone around. I browsed half-heartedly through some pamphlets, wondering if I'd find anything to top the unintentional hilarity and ludicrousness of the ones I'd seen on the bulletin board.

Then I heard a small breeze behind me. Well, I thought it was a breeze, but it was actually a person talking. She spoke so quietly that I didn't even realise she was there.

'I'm sorry?' I asked.

'I said, "Can I help you with anything?"' she asked again, in that drowsy, sing-song, slightly stoned voice which seems to be the compulsory vocal setting for those who reside in the new-age realm.

I told her that she seemed to have a very nice place here and that I was writing about Byron Bay. Would she like to have a chat? She ummed and ahhed and ummed again, and then said yes, and we went to sit out on the verandah. She was Ashiya, the go-to woman if you needed your auras or chakras cleared.

The first thing she told me was this: 'Byron's rotten to the core.'

I was taken aback. This was not what I had expected from someone who dealt with chakras and auras.

I asked her to elaborate.

'It's the council,' she said. 'There are many green issues that are being ignored. At the moment they're spraying herbicides around our streets that they know are affecting people with multiple chemical sensitivities. They use Round-Up. Do you know anything about Round-Up?'

I had to admit that I didn't.

'It's just one step down from Agent Orange.'

Really?

She nodded solemnly, and told me about the group she had set up called ROAR—Residents Organised Against Roundup.

Ashiya was originally from New Zealand. She first visited Byron 15 years ago in a camper van with her kids, then moved here six years ago. For an entire year she lived in her van, parking near the beach or in the rainforest.

'I loved it back then,' she said. 'But in the last six years the community has fragmented. When the war in Iraq started, 45 of us hired a bus and drove to Canberra to protest. I don't think that would happen now. Tourism has changed everything.'

She claimed that a lot of people came to Byron Bay because of the spiritual aspect, even though they may not have been aware of what was bringing them here at the time.

'It's about the vortex energy. Do you know about vortexes?'

Um, no. But I got the feeling I was about to become acquainted with them.

'What about auras and chakras?'

That would be a no, and another no.

'Well, I can see people's auras and I can read them.'

Could she tell I was a complete sceptic? I don't even read my horoscope. I had my palm read for the first time a couple of months previously, but that was for a magazine story as I was writing about the palm reader in question. She had told me that in my past life I was a Spanish swordsman similar to Zorro, that I would live to the age of 84 (shaving at least 50 years off Beautiful Al's prediction), that I would never be attacked by a shark, and that I should not live in a house with cats (at the time I was living in a house with three cats). In other words, she sounded like a crazy lady who was listing random thoughts that happened to cross her mind.

Still, today was my day to embrace the age of Aquarius so against my better judgement I asked Ashiya what my aura was telling her.

She gazed at me.

'You've been drinking a lot of tea,' she said.

I tried to keep a look of interest on my face, as I listened to this less-than-enthralling deduction.

'A lot of tea...or coffee,' she elaborated.

I drink perhaps two cups of coffee and one cup of tea a day. As far as I know this doesn't make me eligible for rehab. But I didn't tell Ashiya this. I just nodded and attempted to look serious.

'There's a certain frequency in your energy field and the caffeine is not good for you. You need to drink more water.'

She looked at me again and was silent for a moment.

'Do you live where there's a lot of pollution?'

Not a lot, I told her. I said that I lived near the beach in Sydney, but I was about to move back to the inner city where I used to live for a decade. And that I'd like to one day live in New York.

'New York will be good for you, actually,' she said immediately, picking up on this. 'It's a more vibrant energy than where you're living now.'

Well, duh, I thought. New York has a more vibrant energy than just about anywhere on the planet so that was no great insight.

'Let me tell you about the vortexes. The planet has chakras, just like people do, and they're called vortexes. Byron is a hotspot for vortexes. We're a little basin surrounded by vortex energy. That's why Byron attracts writers, artists, dancers and healers. They don't even know why they come here sometimes.'

She paused.

I nodded.

She continued.

'And that's why the dolphins are here too. They're riding the songlines. The whales are important because they activate the vortexes in the ocean and they travel along the songlines. The vortexes are what keeps the planet vital and gives it spiritual energy. Do you understand?'

I had absolutely no idea what she was talking about. Like all new-age flim-flam I'd been exposed to, the explanations— if that's what you can call them—were long and winding and convoluted, and appeared to make no sense.

But I just said, 'That's interesting.'

'You know the full story with the war in Iraq, don't you?' she asked.

Um, what's that?

'Well, the whole thing's a conspiracy.'

Uh-oh. Of course I'd heard the conspiracy theories, that the World Trade Centre towers were destroyed by a controlled explosion, that the Pentagon was not hit by a plane, but a missile, that the plane that crashed in Pennsylvania was shot down by the US Airforce. I'd also heard that the moon landing was staged, that there was a triangular area in Bermuda where ships mysteriously disappeared, and that there was a monster that hung out in Loch Ness, all of which used to fascinate me when I was a spotty teenager.

But Ashiya was serious. And humourless. She recounted in some detail the usual theories about 9/11 and the resulting war as if they were reputable and irrefutable evidence.

I felt my aura start to fade, so made excuses to leave. She wished me luck with my writing, and told me that she too was working on a book. It was called *Diary Of A Byron Fringe Dweller.* I wished her luck with hers as well.

* * *

I kept to the back streets and came across a second-hand bookshop run by a refreshingly down-to-earth woman in her 50s. I needed a flakiness break. She had dyed black hair and wore a brightly patterned muu-muu. We got talking about books and then about Byron. I wondered if different nationalities tended to buy certain kinds of books.

'Well, I'm not one to generalise,' she warned. 'But you could say that the English tend to buy beach reads. The Germans and Scandinavians are more interested in literary books. But what really encourages me is that some of the local kids are coming in looking for the Beats and Kurt Vonnegut and Günter Grass. That gives you some hope, doesn't it?'

It certainly does. I bought something (not a beach read) and said goodbye, and soon afterwards saw a sign.

No, I wasn't having a road to Damascus style conversion here. I actually saw a sign. It was on the door of a bakery. Here's what it said:

> Usually we open about 7:30 a.m.
> But sometimes as late as 9 or 10 a.m.
> Or sometimes not at all (Monday).
> Usually we close about 6 p.m.
> But sometimes as early as 3 or 4 p.m.
> Or as late as 5 p.m.
> Some days we don't open.
> Or some afternoons.
> But lately we've been here most of the time except when we've been away.

In many ways, this little sign summed up Byron. Sure, the sign was meant to be funny, and it kind of was, but it was like one of those jokes that went on a bit too long. It was poking a bit of gentle fun at the lackadaisical, laidback nature of their business attitude, but at the same time it was a bit of a hangover of hippy times.

What annoyed me most was that the bakery was closed, because some of the biscuits in there looked quite delicious, and I was hungry.

I decided to have a twirling lesson. Those are seven words I never thought I'd utter in my life.

I saw the ad for the lessons in a shop called Fairy Floss. I wouldn't normally enter a shop with the words Fairy, or indeed, Floss, in the name. But when in Byron, do as the Byronians do.

It was one of those shops that you always seem to find in beachy 'alternative' places. They sold incense and runes and amulets shaped like dolphins or stars. They sold brightly coloured clothing that was baggy and shapeless and had thick stitching that made it look like it was inside-out. Apparently being alternative meant that you couldn't wear sober colours or anything that might vaguely fit the contours of your body. Or anything that looked cool. Instead you had to look like a circus clown crossed with an extra out of *Mad Max*.

The shop also sold twirling sticks that you could light at either end. I'd often looked at fire twirlers—well, let me back up here—I'd often avoided looking at fire twirlers because I've always thought (a) wow, twirling a stick that's on fire at both ends, how fascinating; and (b) anyone could do that, so what's everyone looking at?

I turned up at the park behind the bus station where a group of six had congregated. Our instructor was Mick, a lean, laconic, slightly grizzled guy who I took to be in his late thirties. He might have been 50 or 25 for all I know because every guy I met in Byron seemed to be lean, grizzled and laconic, so it was impossible to ascertain their age. He'd been twirling for five years and only took it up because the teenage daughter of his then partner was into it, and introduced him to it.

Mick asked how much twirling experience I'd had, and after I told him that it was on par with my experience as a neurosurgeon, he decided to start me on the poi. This is a beanbag about the size of a large plum at the end of a length of wire. At the other end is a leather loop through which you lace your fingers.

Mick gave me two poi and started me on the most basic move, standing with my body angled to the left, lifting the poi in the air so they swung up over my head, and then shifting to angle my body to the right as they fell behind me. It sounded ridiculously easy. It took me more than 10 minutes to master. Over the next hour I learned four more moves, getting to the point where I could move the poi in different directions, but for my trouble I developed a series of small beanbag-shaped bruises on my thighs and buttocks. By contrast, the French girl next to me seemed to be ready to audition for Cirque du Soleil.

'Have you been doing this for a long while?' I asked her.

'This is my second lesson,' she said, smiling as one of my poi hit me in the back of the head.

'You've got to learn the basics,' Mick told me. 'And then you keep practising and get to know them so well that you get to the point where you don't even have to think about them anymore. They just come naturally.'

I doubted very much I would get to that point, as I was 99 per cent sure this was my first and last twirling lesson. Not that I told Mick this. It did teach me to appreciate that there was more to fire twirling than just randomly swinging something around a few times and trying not to burn off all your body hair. But I knew I would never progress from poi to sticks. And there was no way I was going to wear baggy orange pants that looked like they were on inside-out.

Halfway along Jonson Street is the place where new blood is infused into Byron Bay every day. Buses arrive from Sydney to the south or from Brisbane and points further north. At the end of the twirling lesson, I stood and watched a bus arrive, the passengers blinking in the sunlight and slightly unsteady on their feet as they hit the pavement after the long journey. There was a chaotic scramble for their backpacks as they were unloaded from the belly of the bus onto the pavement, and then, like seagulls on hot chips, workers from the local hostels, holding clipboards and signs, descended on the backpackers.

Some in the travel industry refer to 'backpacker farming', and watching these people herd the travellers into their minibuses and vans that were parked in a hot vacant lot behind the bus station gave that term a whole new meaning. Within 15 minutes, all the vans were full and had peeled away to their various destinations, leaving the area empty, awaiting the arrival of the next coachload, when the whole process would be repeated.

I walked back down Jonson Street towards the beach and met Evitsa. He was a taxi driver who was sitting on his haunches on the footpath, waiting for a fare. He had close-cropped hair, a stubbly beard, and wore aviator sunglasses. Like many people I met in Byron, he didn't define himself by what he did to make money.

He said that he drove a cab to feed himself, but in the morning he was a yogi, and at night he was a practitioner of aikido, one of the martial arts. He talked about spirituality, but wasn't airy-fairy about it. He seemed grounded and didn't proselytise or vague out.

He'd been driving in Byron for nine months now. I wondered aloud about how hard a living that must be around here. Byron had a small population, and surely everyone that lived here would either be within walking distance from where they needed to go, or they owned a car. And any backpackers would be too cheap to spring for a cab.

He shrugged and admitted it was a bit slow today, but things could turn. He got his best fare around six months ago, when a group of Irish guys wanted to go to Nimbin to buy marijuana.

'I dropped them there, had some lunch, and then took them back an hour later after they scored their weed,' he said. 'I got 300 bucks for the round trip. They offered me some weed, too, but I don't smoke.'

Evitsa was born in Macedonia and grew up in Sydney. He'd been coming to Byron for 12 years, before finally moving here 18 months ago.

'The thing people have in common here is a free spirit,' he said. 'That may mean they want to be active from dusk till dawn, or it may mean they want to drink beer and watch TV. When I first came here, there were a lot more hippies. Not anymore. It's too expensive. There are a lot more people with money now. But you have to accept that about Byron. This is the yuppie phase we're in now, but it'll move on eventually.'

Did he really think that things would change and Byron could become a hippy haven again?

'Everything changes. Even now, there's just this natural process where the wrong people for Byron end up leaving. They might come here for the pussy or the partying or whatever, but they don't last. The ones who are meant to be here stay. It's like natural selection.'

And with that, Evitsa took his leave. He had a fare.

I suddenly realised I was starving so I went off in search a place that would fit in with my spiritual search. And I found it down the end of a tacky arcade—a Hare Krishna restaurant.

'What can I serve you today?' asked the girl behind the counter. She had a round, friendly face and she was beaming. But it wasn't one of those 'I've just joined a cult, please help me' kind of looks. She seemed genuine.

I ordered some food, which was simple but delicious, and sat at a table near the window. A skinny guy in his mid-twenties came in. He was wearing torn jeans and had a scruffy beard.

'What can I serve you today?' asked the girl behind the counter.

He was actually wondering if there was any work. There wasn't. A kitchen-hand position had just been filled the day before. The guy looked crestfallen. He also looked hungry. He was dreamily scanning the food on display.

'But look, since you've come in, why don't you sit down and have some food?' she asked.

He indicated that he had no money, and she shook her hand in a half-wave that was a non-verbal signal for 'don't worry about it'. She then realised that she knew him.

'You're Russell, right?'

He confirmed this.

'Riiiight,' she said. 'I know Isaac. Have you heard from Isaac?'

He hadn't seen him for six months now.

'I hope he's all right. I send my prayers out to him. There you are. Enjoy.'

He thanked her and sat down to eat at the table next to me. A couple of minutes later, when a group of three people finished up and left, he hurried over to gather up their plates and take them in to the kitchen, eager to pay the girl back in some way.

'Thanks so much, brother,' she said, making more out of it for his benefit.

She noticed me noticing this and gave me a shy smile. It felt good just seeing a bit of goodness without any ulterior motive. It was a genuine interaction between people, where one was helping another while trying to not make him feel bad or needy as a result of it. It wasn't something you saw very often in the world, and it seemed that even in Byron it wasn't as common as it used to be.

Walking back out onto Jonson Street, I saw some market stalls selling jewellery and clothes and knick-knacks. One stall was offering temporary tattoos. I'd never wanted a tattoo in my life, temporary or otherwise. So naturally, as it seemed the perfect way to finish my new-age day, I decided to get one.

On the underside of my left forearm I got the Japanese symbol for patience, as I felt that was a commodity I was going to need a lot of before the month was over.

Patience cost ten bucks. It started to fade the next morning, and was completely gone three days later.

The following morning, I moved. On my day of flakiness I made enquiries at Cape Byron Hostel, one of the main places in town, and they finally had beds available. A change is as good as a holiday and a change while you're on holiday is better still.

So I checked out of the Belongil Hostel and got talking to Michael, the friendly guy who ran the place. He said it was a fact that Byron had gone from being a town that was 'serious hippyville' to a place that was more concerned with money and less tolerant of people without money.

'Byron has definitely changed, and I don't think it's changed for the better,' he said. 'There's now a more aggressive nature to the place. Even my mum's afraid to go to town after dark. She's been chased after getting money from the ATM. And then you get things like the Rex Hunt incident.'

Rex Hunt is a former Australian Rules footballer and policeman who became an Australian media personality due to his television fishing program and his football commentary on radio. In October 2005, he said he and his son had been the subject of an unprovoked attack by a gang of teenagers outside the Beach Hotel. He claimed they were taunting him as a tourist before they attacked him, slashing his head with a glass and then kicking and punching his son.

The teenagers' story was quite different. They claimed that both Hunt and his son were very drunk, and that his son threw the first punch, hitting one of the group from behind. They said that Rex Hunt's injuries to the head came not from one of them smashing him with a glass, but from Hunt's own daughter-in-law, who was trying to hit the teenagers with the stiletto heel of one of her shoes, but accidentally connected with her father-in-law's head.

Who to believe? Celebrities and teenagers both make notoriously unreliable witnesses in my book. But afterwards it came to light that most of the teenagers were actually straight edge, eschewing alcohol and drugs—on television they even displayed tattoos (of the permanent kind) that read 'My Promise To My Family' and 'Drug Free'.

It also emerged that Hunt would not make an official report to police, despite them asking. This didn't stop him going on current affairs TV to criticise the teenagers and Byron Bay in general. He infamously said he'd feel safer in Bali than Byron Bay, a comment that was no doubt designed to hurt the town's tourism industry. Coming only three years after 88 Australians were killed in the Bali bombings, it was seen by many as a comment that not only exaggerated what happened to him that night, but was incredibly insensitive.

But the point is that despite all the vortexes and songlines and whales and dolphins, Byron isn't all peace and love and brown rice anymore. What's not in dispute is the fact that no matter who started it, violence occurred that night. The mayor, Jan Barham, and the chairman of the chamber of commerce, Greg Owens, were adamant that tourists were not targeted in Byron, although Owens' comment that they were the 'lifeblood' of the place was perhaps not so well chosen considering some of that blood was on the footpath in Jonson Street. And the very next night after this, it was reported that another man had been attacked by seven men, reportedly locals. Apparently a friend went to the man's aid and was smashed in the face with a glass for his trouble.

For Michael at Belongil Backpackers, it was just another facet of the changing face of the place. He'd even seen a shift in the area of spirituality.

'I move in meditation circles but I've noticed there's this me-me-me element in Byron now,' he said. 'The values are very superficial. Even the spiritual centres here have become international and corporate. You go to the real zen centres and they're empty. No one wants the real thing anymore. About five years ago I noticed this narcissism creeping in.'

Speaking of superficial values, as I was waiting for my breakfast in the café attached to the hostel I open up the *Byron Shire News,* and there was a picture of Tara Reid, the actress who starred in the teen comedy film *American Pie,* and has since maintained her fame by drinking a lot, falling over, exposing her breasts in public and becoming a professional party girl. The article breathlessly outlined her upcoming visit to Byron Bay for a magazine photo shoot.

It referred to her as Tara 'Tiara' Reid, noting that she 'partied into the wee hours' at Magic Millions, an annual thoroughbred horse auction held on the Gold Coast, and was due to stay at Byron On Byron, a lavish resort and spa set in 45 acres of land outside of town.

The story went into some detail about the fact she was a size 6, much to the surprise of a swimwear designer, who had mistakenly sent size 8 bikinis for the photo shoot. This development was so engrossing that I almost fell asleep reading it. And I wondered if a publicist had something to do with placing the story to ensure that the public knew Tara wasn't becoming a fat pig who could just squeeze into a size 8. The new narcissism was alive and well in Byron Bay.

Soon afterwards I learned, via a nearby TV, that Byron still had some catching up to do. A commercial news bulletin had a report on Snoop Dogg, the pipecleaner-thin US rapper who had visited Bondi Beach the day before. On the screen, he was barely visible through his security detail, men of such bulk that they obviously had to import a lot more hamburgers, beer and other bulk protein into the area to keep them alive. It was a pity that the satirical TV show *The Chaser's War On Everything* wasn't filming at the time as I would have loved one of their team to dress up as a council ranger and fine the Dogg's minders for not having their charge on a leash.

As he was on Bondi Beach, Mr Dogg had to have the necessary skinny blonde accessory. She came in the shape of Sophie Monk, a former member of manufactured girl group, Bardot. Since that band's implosion in 2002 she had mainly kept a profile by making appearances at openings, disrobing for men's magazines, and getting engaged to a member of pop-punk group Good Charlotte. So when the 'news' reporter breathlessly referred to her as a 'Hollywood actress', it made perfect sense. This was Bondi, where appearances and front were what mattered, not reality. Her two biggest roles to date, just in case you missed them, were as a bimbo in the Adam Sandler movie *Click,* and 'parodying' a famous bimbo in *Date Movie.*

Which famous bimbo was she parodying? Paris Hilton, of course, who had caused even more chaos in Bondi just a couple of weeks beforehand.

My new home, the Cape Byron Hostel, was two blocks from Jonson Street and two blocks back from the main beach. The rooms were arranged around a fenced-off swimming pool and barbecue area, giving the place a 1970s motel feel.

When I arrived, three girls were lying on white plastic banana lounges around the pool. One was talking into a mobile phone and the other two are smoking and chatting in northern English accents. All three were very white. My guess was they'd only been in town for an hour, and they wouldn't be white for long. I walked into my room and the first person I met was an English guy named Rob.

'If you like partying and you don't like to sleep too much, you've come to the right hostel,' he informed me. 'And this room is the number one place for partying.'

Excellent. I discovered that there were two Englishmen, an Israeli, a Canadian, an Italian, a German and three Swedes in here.

Patrick, from Stuttgart, was sitting outside the door with his back to the wall, next to his surfboard. He planned on staying in Byron for four days. That was four weeks ago.

'Byron is that kind of place,' he said. 'I rented a surfboard for three days and after that I loved it so much I bought this one. I'm only in Australia for three months, and I've spent one third of this time here.'

He shook his head.

'I just don't want to leave. But now I have to sell my board, get a bus back to Sydney tomorrow and fly to Tasmania.'

There were so many Germans in Sydney that he wondered if there were any left back at home. Part of the reason he wanted to come to Australia, apart from the surfing, was to practise his English, so he didn't just want to hang out with his countrymen. He was studying English literature and physical education in Stuttgart and he wanted to become a teacher.

As we were talking, a bronzed guy wearing nothing but Speedos and a cowboy hat walked up. He was holding a pool cue and had a cigarette in the side of his mouth.

'Patrick?' he asked, looking at both of us.

'That's me,' said Patrick.

'I'm here about the board.'

He had a quick look at the surfboard, nodded, and handed over five $50 notes.

'I'll take care of her for you,' he said, 'But can you keep her here for a while longer? I've got to finish my pool game.'

And with that, the Speedo Cowboy ambled back to the pool table.

'I need this,' said Patrick, fanning out the $50 notes. 'But I'll miss her.'

And then he literally kissed his board goodbye, planting his lips on the waxed fibreglass. Meanwhile, I had an appointment with a newspaper man.

'I'm a newcomer,' Gary Chigwidden said. 'I've been here 24 years. You have to be here at least 30 years before they call you a local. But as newcomers go, I'm one of the older newcomers.'

Gary is the editor of the *Byron Shire News*. He arrived here from Sydney in 1983 to open café called Savoir Fare ('I got sick of explaining to people that I knew it wasn't spelt correctly and that it was a play on words.'). He and his wife were looking to leave Sydney and saw an ad in the *Sydney Morning Herald* for a café in Byron.

'I'd never even been to Byron before. We got here on a Friday night and the next morning drove up in the old Belmont to Main Beach. It was the middle of winter and there were only two other cars in the carpark. It was an absolutely magic, sunny day and I remember looking at the beach and up to the cape and thinking, 'Shit, this'll do me."

He laughed and picked at the packed lunch on his desk.

'I'm not a cosmic navel-gazing person, but it just felt like I was born to come here. I felt like I'd come home.'

The same year he arrived in Byron, the meatworks closed down, 400 people were put out of work, and 'the town went into mourning'.

'That changed when John Cornell built the Beach Hotel. Before that it was the Seabreeze Hotel. God, that was rough. A real bloodhouse. Full of bikies. He transformed the place. A lot of the ferals and alternative lifers moved to the hinterland, to Nimbin and Mullumbimby—not that there was anything wrong with them. People liked them. But Byron was becoming more of a holiday town and tourism became the major industry.'

The base population of Byron is just over 9000, yet up to 1.7 million tourists come here every year. Peak times on the calendar include two music festivals (The East Coast Blues And Roots Music Festival at Easter, and Splendour in the Grass in July), Christmas and New Year's Eve, and Schoolies Week, when the town is overrun for a fortnight in November by school-leavers. It's a time of alcoholic over-indulgence, non-stop partying and fumbling sex. Gary acknowledged that Byron was not the most pleasant place to live at these times, 'but if you're going to live here, you have to realise that's what happens. You have to accept it because you live in such a great place.'

But did he ever think back to that idyllic day in 1983 when he sat in his Belmont and said, 'Shit, this'll do me'?

'You know what?' he said. 'I say basically nothing's changed. The good things I fell in love with on that first day are still here. The beaches and the cape are still here. And the things that weren't so good, like lack of shopping facilities and lack of work opportunities, those have expanded remarkably.

'You talk to any genuine local here, who has lived here for decades, and they think Byron is great now. I talk to those people and say, 'Wasn't it a great place to grow up?' And they say, 'Yeah, I guess it was okay but there was nothing to do."

*   *   *

Back at the hostel many of the residents seemed to be taking 'nothing to do' as their personal creed. The same three English girls were still lying on the same three banana lounges. They looked pinker than they did when I left. A different one was on the phone this time. The other two were chatting and smoking. Perhaps they were a British slothfulness relay team, passing the phone between each other at intervals, like a baton.

I'm not the most sporty of characters, but sometimes watching others do nothing can spur a guy on. For a few days I'd wanted to climb Cape Byron and visit the lighthouse, so I decided there was no time like the present. I also just felt like being a regular tourist in Byron Bay for a little while instead of talking to every single person I met to get their story.

Why not just go for a nice walk? Well, why not?

It was already after lunch when I set off, so after wandering down Main Beach, I went for a bodysurf at Clarkes Beach, sat on the sand for a while watching the surfers and then walked further along to the Pass, where long, slow waves bend around the cape. From here there's a gap in the bushland where I found a path leading up and across the headland. A short, hot climb and descent revealed Watego's Beach, one of the treasures of Byron. Although it's not very far away, the fact that it's separated from the main beach means that few backpackers bother venturing this far. As a result it's much less crowded, despite the fact that it has a naturally secluded setting and great surf.

I immediately went into the water and caught more waves in half an hour than I had in two days. There was a handful of guys in their forties and fifties riding longboards down the right-hand end of the beach, where the waves keep rolling for ages before finally breaking. These guys had all the time in the world to catch them and ride them all the way in to shore, walking backwards and forwards along their boards for balance, as the wave kept rolling on and on.

There was one guy with matted blond hair who did this with the ease and grace of a loose-limbed ape. He'd switch from a natural stance (left foot forward) to goofy (right foot forward), crabwalking to the front of the board to place his toes on the nose, then slowly scuffling back, finally sitting on his board as if he was on his lounge room floor watching television, and then casually pulling off the wave. At the end there there were no whoops of joy, no punching the air, no communal high-fives. He just paddled out again on his knees with long scoops of his arms, and then sat there waiting for another wave. Because there's always another wave.

As I watched him catch one wave after another, I thought that he approached surfing like the people here seemed to approach living—unhurried, not hassled, no sudden movements, with an off-handedness that said, 'What? Me surfing? Well, yeah, I guess you could say that's what I'm doing. I hadn't really thought about it to tell you the truth.'

I picked up the path again at the other end of the beach and kept walking as it rounded the cape and twisted to the right. Up ahead there were people pointing into the water below. I reached them, looked down, and there were dark shapes moving in the ocean that, on closer inspection, turned out to be turtles and stingrays.

A little further along was a sign indicating that this was the most easterly point in mainland Australia. If you were planning on swimming to the United States as a result of delusions of grandeur or just plain grand delusion, this would be the place to start. Up the hill was the lighthouse itself, which has a lens that weighs 8 tons and has a power—so it said in the information booklet I found up there—of 2,200,000 candelas. No, I didn't know the unit of luminous intensity was the candela either. And yes, apparently a standard candle emits one candela of intensity. A 100-watt lightbulb emits about 120. So imagine 18,333 lightbulbs concentrated in one spot and that's how bright the beam from Cape Byron lighthouse is. The light travels as far as 40 kilometres.

From the woman who had the enviable job of sitting up there reading a book, looking at the view, and occasionally answering questions from curious visitors, I discovered that the lighthouse was meant to be opened by the then premier of New South Wales, John See, in 1901. Ironically, the boat on which he'd travelled from Sydney couldn't land because of rough weather, even though he could quite clearly see the thing he was meant to be opening, as the beam lit up the ocean all around Byron Bay. Legend has it that he performed an 'acrobatic feat' on hitting dry land, was informed that the banquet and ceremony had gone ahead without him the previous night, and then he and his party repaired to the great

Northern Hotel in town to make up for lost time. Politicians certainly sounded like more fun back in those days.

On the way back down from the lighthouse I spotted a pod of nine dolphins, stopped for another excellent swim at Watego's, and then saw an ice-cream truck pull up. I hadn't bought an ice-cream from an ice-cream truck in years. This was turning out to be a storybook kind of day.

The ice-cream man was shaped like a guy who obviously liked to take a lot of his work home with him, and he was sitting on a fence in front of the truck, looking a little wistfully at the surf. He smiled when I walked up.

'Wouldn't be dead for quids on a day like this, would you, brother?'

I certainly wouldn't. I bought an ice-cream cone with a chocolate Flake in it and headed back in the direction of Byron. I felt like a kid and it felt good.

When I got back, the three English girls were still on the banana lounges. The sun was low in the sky but it had done its work. The girls were glowing red. I sat at a table nearby, taking some notes from the day, and one of them struck up a conversation.

'What did you get up to today, then?' she asked.

I told her all about my walk to the lighthouse and the great beach at Watego's and the stingrays and the turtles and the dolphins.

'Oh yeah,' she said, and I could swear she was trying to suppress a yawn. 'We read something about that in *Lonely Planet*, but it looks too far away.'

'It's really not,' I told her. 'And it's worth the walk. You should give it a try while you're here.'

'Yeah, I dunno.'

'If you're not satisfied, blame me.'

'But we're on holiday!' she said, her voice rising. 'What would we wanna walk all that way when we've got a pool right here?'

It was certainly hard to argue with logic like that. Especially from someone who looked like a cooked lobster. Although they had barely moved all day, she and her two companions would be living in a world of pain later tonight.

I am dancing on a table. I have no fear of being thrown out of the particular establishment where I have chosen to do this because everyone else is also dancing on a table. If I wasn't dancing on a table here, a gorilla-sized guy with no neck and an earpiece would come up to me and say, 'Excuse me, sir, but unless you plan to dance on a table, I'm afraid I'm going to have to ask you to leave. And make some goddamn noise while you're at it.'

You know those scenes in American teen movies of the 1980s where the characters walk into some bar that is pumping with bad dance music and a couple of guys walk past wearing—I don't know—let's say sombreros, and a bunch of girls walk the other way with their hands in the air squealing 'woooooo-hooooo!' and then the camera pans around and there are masses of people dancing on tables and also squealing 'woooooo-hooooo!'? You see those scenes in movies and think, 'Why don't movies ever get club scenes right? I've never once walked into a place that looks like that.'

Well, go to Cheeky Monkey's in Byron Bay and you'll discover you were wrong because that scene—sombreros and all—exactly describes what happened the night I wandered in.

And just as Nancy Sinatra's boots were made for walking, the tables at Cheeky Monkey's were made for dancing. They looked like they were designed for prisons. They were thick and sturdy and made of steel with bumps on it. Imagine a manhole cover, but shiny and stretched into a rectangle a couple of metres long and that's your bit of the dance floor for the night.

These tables were congregated in an area at the back of the bar, surrounded by banks of video screens. There was bumping, there was grinding, there was much sucking of beers, there was much skulling of shots, and…there appeared to be some heavy frottage going on at a corner table.

'Woooo-hoooooo!' screamed the guy dancing opposite me. His name was Alex and he was from Israel.

'Woooo-hoooooo!' I replied, after failing to come up with anything else intelligent to say.

This was the most animated I had seen Alex. He was one of my room-mates, he spoke in a droning monotone, and he didn't understand irony or have a sense of humour. Admittedly I'd only known him a matter of hours at that point, but he didn't appear to ever smile. Even while screaming 'Woooo-hoooooo!' he had a certain seriousness about him, which was a pretty mean feat.

Earlier in the evening Alex had suggested we go to the Beach Hotel. While the DJ took us on an archaeological dig through one-hit wonders of the past few decades (progressing from The Knack's 'My Sharona' to Deee-Lite's 'Groove is in the Heart' to EMF's 'Unbelievable'), Alex and I talked about women. Well, Alex did. It was more of a monologue than a conversation.

He said that all Israeli girls turn into sluts when they travel, even if they're not like that at home. He said that Canadian girls 'will fuck you in an alleyway at two in the morning after you've known them for half an hour'. And he said that if it was late in the night and his luck wasn't with him, then he'd try only chatting up fat or ugly girls (or what he considered to be fat and ugly girls) because 'they're always up for being banged'.

He was a real charmer. And he said all this with no relish, just with that same expressionless monotone. I got the feeling my new acquaintance hadn't had much luck in the relationship department.

After a couple of beers he suggested we go to Cheeky Monkey's, 'because they all dance on the tables and get very drunk there, so there is a good chance that I will be able to find a girl to bang'.

His use of the word 'bang' was really starting to worry me, but I figured it was going to be really loud at Cheeky Monkey's, so I wouldn't be able to hear him say it again.

And besides, I really wanted to dance on a table.

You want to know what it's like? It's like dancing on the ground, but about a metre higher, more crowded, and there's always a possibility that you're going to fall off. Pretty exciting stuff.

Because there are eight or ten or twelve people crammed onto each rectangle of steel, you can't help but get up close and personal with your fellow table-top dwellers, which is how I met Anna.

She was 23 years old, she came from Germany, and she was a breath of fresh air, mainly because she was actually doing something on her holiday other than sitting by a swimming pool in a banana lounge every day. In fact, she had bought a Ford panel van for $2200, christened it Trevor, and was in the process of driving it around the country.

She arrived in Sydney six months ago and had held down two waitressing jobs in Bondi. She had done fruit-picking and sorting in Innesfail, waking up at 4:30 every morning in a workers hostel that was overrun with cockroaches and frogs, and keeping an eye out for spiders while sorting bananas (a Swedish girl she was working with was bitten). She'd started a relationship with an Australian from Airlie Beach and lived with him for a month, but then discovered he was a depressive alcoholic with violent moodswings and had to leave. Driving from there to Gladstone she stopped for petrol and was propositioned by a truck driver who offered her money for sex. Despite all this, she remained resolutely upbeat and had no regrets about her trip, continuing to travel alone, often through isolated areas of Australia.

She was staying at a different hostel, but after we left Cheeky Monkey's and before parting ways, we went down to the water and sat on the grass for a while outside the Beach Hotel, watching the lighthouse's beam sweep past every 15 seconds.

'How far do you think the light goes?' Anna asked.

And, of course, I knew the answer. If she'd asked me 24 hours earlier I would have had no idea. It pays to climb hills and ask questions.

A few months previously, *Forbes Traveler* magazine published its list of the 25 sexiest beaches in the world. Even they had the good grace to say that although the decision was difficult, the task was not the most onerous they'd ever undertaken.

Some of the usual suspects made the list—Copacabana, Saint-Tropez, South Beach. But Waikiki didn't make it and neither did Bondi. Both too overcrowded, according to the hard-working *Forbes Traveler* researchers.

The results of this highly scientific study were apparently based on a scale that involved 'that special combination of sensuality, sassiness and scenic beauty', empirical qualities that I don't recall entering into in my chemistry and physics classes at school. The magazine included input from travel writers, tour planners, marine biologists, meteorologists, cultural essayists, and 'personal diarists devoted to covering the beach scene'. This last group sounded like a euphemism for 'beach bums' or possibly 'dole bludgers'.

Anyway, only one Australian beach made it onto the list, and that was Byron Bay. The judges praised its 'chalk-white sands and deliciously temperate weather and occasional visits from dolphins and migrating whales.'

I'd like to think that I lowered Byron's 'sexiest beach' rating every time I ventured onto the sand, and decided to really give their ranking a beating by hiring a surfboard and hanging around for six hours.

I didn't initially intend to stay there for six hours, but a combination of my (perhaps misplaced) determination to once and for all master the art of standing on a surfboard while on a wave, along with my obvious lack of qualities in the departments marked balance, skill and physical endurance, meant that I was in for the long haul.

The first hour was a wash-out, unless I was being judged for a perfect impersonation of an old guy drowning while clutching a stick of fibreglass, in which case I deserved an Oscar. To add to my shame, three kids whose combined ages were still less than mine, were regularly whizzing past me, not only standing up with ease, but cutting backwards and forwards across the face of the waves, and making annoyingly gleeful noises while doing it.

I retreated to the sand for a while to catch my breath, rest my tired limbs and to decide whether to continue. Back in the water, I was joined by a teenage girl on a board decorated with a red flower pattern. We got talking and she said she'd only been learning for a couple of weeks. Despite this, she caught waves at a ratio of roughly 20:1 compared to me. I told her—quite unnecessarily considering the form I was showing out there—that I'd had one lesson in my life and this was my first time as a solo wanna-be.

'It's just practice,' she said. 'I've been coming out here every day for two weeks. After three or four days something clicked and now it feels more natural, you know? But I saw you standing up before, so that's pretty good if you're only out for the second time.'

'Standing up' was gilding the lily somewhat. I had vaguely got to my feet a few times, usually for a handful of seconds before falling off, or nosediving then falling off, or overbalancing backwards and falling off. Once I actually fell off the board while just trying to sit on it. This wasn't the most dignified of moves, and I sheepishly looked around when my head emerged to see that my new surfing buddy was only 5 metres away. God bless her, she pretended not to notice.

After her small words of encouragement, something miraculous happened. I magically started to get it together on the very next wave. I waited for the wave to surge beneath me before pushing down with my arms on the board and I got to my feet at just the right point. And I stood up. Not just for 1 second or 5 seconds. I rode it until it lost power and then I flicked off.

Underwater I let out a bubbly yell that was equal parts triumph and relief. I was hooked. I took just a few breaks to rest and to eat and drink, but I didn't leave the beach for the whole day, eager to keep going until I had to return the board at six o'clock. Finally I hobbled up the beach at 5:45, lugging my board back to the surf shop.

'How'd you go?' asked the girl at the counter.

'Not bad,' I said, trying to look as casual as possible.

'Yeah, a bit small today,' she said. 'Easy waves, though.'

Yeah, right. Really easy. I wandered back to the hostel in an exhausted daze, but I felt clean and salty and fitter than I had in ages. My muscles felt tight. No, I felt like I actually had muscles. This was new. I also realised that I was aching all over. My neck, shoulders and arms throbbed from all the paddling. I noticed that there were angry red welts on my stomach from board rash, and my knees stung because I'd grazed the skin on the sand after crashing out a couple of times.

Most of these aches, pains and grazes would fade over the next couple of days. One doesn't.

'Let's smoke the weed.'

'Have you got the weed?'

'Yeah, of course I've got the weed.'

'Where should we smoke the weed?'

'Should we smoke the weed on the roof?'

This exchange went on for some time outside the room, in the series of hoarse whispers backpackers always seem to use in the small hours of the morning, thinking that they're being very quiet and considerate, when in fact they may as well be using loudhailers, as they go on and on, and everyone can hear every word.

I was in bed. It was one in the morning. After my day of surfing it felt like someone had scrubbed my bones with steel wool and pummelled every muscle in my body with a mallet, while applying a naked flame to the skin on my nose and odd patches of my lower back, behind my knees and on top of my feet, where the sunblock either didn't reach or had rubbed off. All I wanted to do was sleep for the next eight hours, but all this talk of 'the weed' made me think that I needed to get up and investigate.

So I emerged, blinking in the fluorescent light outside our room. There I found a bunch of my room-mates congregated with a cask of goon, some beers, a battered acoustic guitar and what looked like a cake box.

'Did someone mention some weed?' I asked.

'Yeah, man,' said a tall Swedish guy with matted black hair, who was holding the guitar in one hand and an apple in the other. 'We were going on the roof but I think we'll just sit in there next to the pool. Wanna come?'

'Sure,' I said.

We climbed the fence, as the gate was locked. This area was officially out of bounds at night. I felt like I was about 13 years old. There were eight of us parked around a picnic table—three Swedish guys, a Swedish girl, an English guy, an English girl, and a Canadian guy.

Oskar was a dreadlocked Swede who was carrying the cake box. He opened it up and there was an entire chocolate cake in there, which he proceeded to devour with a plastic fork. Between mouthfuls he told everyone about the best concert he had ever seen in his life—former Pink Floyd mainman Roger Waters at the Roskilde Festival.

'He played the whole of *Dark Side Of The Moon*,' said Oskar. 'I was almost crying at the end.'

'Was it really that bad?' I asked.

The others got the joke, but Oskar was serious.

'It was so good that I wanted him to play it over again when he finished. The 1980s ruined music, man.'

'How old are you?' I asked him.

'Twenty,' he said.

He was born 14 years after *Dark Side Of The Moon* was released. He idolised a guy whose main audience were in their fifties and sixties. He was so young that he should have been into music that I, a guy over twice his age, should have never heard of, or found outrageous, or both.

At least the English guy and the Swedish girl were upholding their side of things as young people of the early 21st century. They were feeling each other up under the table. That was more like it.

Meanwhile, the Canadian was fumbling around for the chords to Oasis's 'Wonderwall', which is to the backpacker night-time singalong what 'Kumbayah' used to be to scout troops around the campfire. Alas, he was mangling it so badly that everyone started complaining and asking someone else to take over.

'I think I can play it,' I said, and soon we were singing along to Noel Gallagher's touching lyrics, comparing his then girlfriend to a bunch of bricks. Ignoring Oskar's pleas for 'Another Brick In The Wall', I managed to pull off requests for Nirvana's 'Smells Like Teen Spirit', REM's 'Losing My Religion' and The Ramones' 'I Wanna Be Sedated', and was rewarded with a hit from the apple.

Yes, they made a bong out of a piece of fruit. It had a hole punctured through the skin on one side. The pot was lit in the indent where the stalk used to be, and then you sucked the smoke through the hole. It tasted bitter, with an aftertaste of Granny Smith and traces of the Coolabah cask wine from the mouth of the previous smoker. Although I admit I'm totally lame in the drug-taking department, even in my limited experience I would say that this was a fairly dismal way to get a low-grade high.

The call went up for some AC/DC, so I cranked out the riff to 'TNT'. The massed backing shouts of 'oi' and the yelling of the celebratory line 'watch me explode!' were finally too much for one backpacker. He emerged from his room, his face red with anger. He was so apoplectic with rage that he was barely coherent, but the salient facts appeared to be these: it's 2:30 in the fucking morning, people are trying to fucking sleep, you're making a fucking noise, so shut the fuck up. Or words to that effect.

So we decided to shut the fuck up. After one more verse and a double chorus. At that moment I no longer felt like I was 13 years old. I felt like I was about eight.

The next morning I woke up with the taste of apple, smoke and goon in my mouth. I opened my eyes and there in the bunk opposite was the Swedish girl from last night, being spooned by the English guy she was with. They were both asleep. He was bare chested and wearing boxer shorts; she had the sheet up under her armpits.

They looked strangely sweet and innocent. I looked at them and thought how touching it seemed. In that minute all the bullshit, the bravado, the bone-headedness and the buffoonery of the backpacker lifestyle melted away. They were just two young travellers in their early twenties, off in dreamland, content in the closeness and the warmth of each other's bodies, and the secret thrill of finding each other, even if it was only for one night.

Man, what was in that apple bong?

Of course, they would wake up in an hour or three, and everything could well be ruined. The spell would be broken. They'd have to speak.

But for that moment, the foot odour, the farts, the sweat, the smoke and the alcohol faded. I even warded off the impending hangover for 10 minutes.

Carina was not surly, blasé or rude. How she got a job as a backpacker hostel receptionist without possessing any of these qualities remains a mystery.

She was always friendly, constantly smiling, talkative with everyone, and eager to help with anything at all you might need. She was also insanely attractive, immaculately made up, and always dressed in clothing that accentuated her Latino shapeliness. If she had said that straight after her shift she was off to take part in Miss World, representing her home country of Brazil, I would have believed her.

Byron wasn't quite penetrating my cynical outer shell, so when I say this, please don't think I've gone off with the pixies—she had a certain aura around her that read 'I'm a good person, and after speaking with me for 5 minutes, you too will feel good'. And that, as we have already learned, is coming from someone who doesn't believe in auras.

She also had a backstory like a Pedro Almodovar heroine. Suffice to say she left Sao Paolo at the age of 20 and went off to see the world, only to meet and marry a Greek man 18 years her senior, who turned out to have a shocking gambling habit. The money disappeared, quickly followed by the marriage vows. Now, at the age of 32, she was happily married to an Australian, and had been living in Byron for the last six years.

As she'd worked here at Cape Byron Hostel for the last three years, I asked her about national stereotypes and if there was any truth in them.

'My favourite people are the Americans,' she said.

Really?

She smiled.

'No. My experience has been bad every time. They're obnoxious and dumb. And they expect you to do everything for them. The Japanese and Koreans are very polite and pleasant and sweet. I used to think badly of Israelis, but I changed my mind. When they first talk to you, you think they're rude, but after a while you realise it's just their manner, and they don't mean it. Italians are a good laugh and I connect with them.

'Irish are the biggest piss-heads, and the funny thing is they don't even know how to drink. They're just out of control and they don't know when to stop. We've had to kick some of them out of here.

'But the young Australians who come to the hostel are bad too. They don't care about rules, and they get drunk and use the pool when they're not meant to and make lots of noise.'

I blushed a little. Although there was no way I could be classified as a 'young' Australian, about ten hours ago I was definitely where I shouldn't have been, and making a hell of a lot of noise.

'Most backpackers want to get pissed and laid,' said Carina. 'But that's okay, right? It's the age. Can you blame them?'

She said that she'd seen changes even in the half dozen years she'd been here.

'There are many more shops, but not enough people to keep them going. There's more people in Byron, but they don't have a lot of money to spend. And of course during Schoolies and on New Year's Eve I don't like Byron, but that's only for a short time of the year.

'I love Byron the rest of the time. Nobody's stressed, the lifestyle's so chilled, and you get to know all the people. It's brought out my softer side. Now if I see a snake in my backyard, I go, 'Oh, isn't it sweet?' Or if I see a tree being cut down I feel like crying. Byron has changed me. I don't plan to ever leave.'

Some talk about the good old days of Byron, that long-ago era of the 1960s and 1970s, when new arrivals rolled into town in beaten-up Kombi vans rather than gleaming BMW four-wheel drives. They fondly reminisce about simpler times when the place was home to hippies and surfers and drop-outs, people who were seeking adventure and the simple life, not real estate and a resort lifestyle, or a transplanted version of their old city life in slightly more idyllic surroundings.

But some can look back even further than 30 or 40 years. They have ancestors that hung out in Byron over 20,000 years ago. The Aboriginal Bundjalung people knew of a Byron Bay not just before the Beach Hotel arrived, but before white men even set eyes on the place and thought, 'Hmmm, nice right-hand point break over there, park the Kombi and let's try it out'.

The two Bundjalung clans most associated with the area are the Arkwal and the Minjunbal, who have recently been recognised by the NSW government as custodians of land in Byron Bay. But even many in the Aboriginal community acknowledge that despite being custodians, no one can actually lay claim to owning Byron.

The Arkwal name for Byron Bay is 'cavanbah', which means meeting place. As the most easterly point of Australia, it was always seen as a place where different tribes gathered to meet each other in a safe environment, to undertake ceremonies and 'make lore', and then move on.

In February 2007, NSW Premier Morris Iemma took the trip from Sydney to Byron and then up the hill to the lighthouse, where he ratified two agreements with the Bundjalung people, acknowledging their custodianship of over 245 hectares of local land.

'I feel really welcome here, really safe here,' said Napier Walters, one of the Bundjalung men at the ceremony. 'It takes away a lot of heartache, a lot of pain.'

The Premier commented that he was meant to be in Canberra preparing for the summit on water with the Prime Minister and other state and territory premiers, but felt this was more important. The cynic in me immediately saw this as a point-scoring comment that was meant to say, 'look at me, I'm a good guy for hanging out here with Aboriginal people and offering at least some recognition that we basically stole the place from them a couple of hundred years ago'.

But then Iemma looked at the view from the lighthouse, that sweeping crescent of white sand and blue water stretching below from the headland on one side, and the expanse of ocean on the other, where turtles, stingrays and dolphins could be seen. And he said, 'It's the most beautiful press conference I'm ever likely to go to.'

Byron Bay even gets to politicians. It makes everyone a bit softer, a bit more reflective, a bit more hippy. But I was with the Bundjalung—Byron was a place to hang out, meet people, enjoy what it had to offer, and then move on.

I took one last look at the beach and hobbled off to the bus station, my body aching under the weight of my backpack. I was riding the dog again, heading further north, and crossing the border.

ANSWER FROM PAGE 107: Earthing is complete nonsense. As opposed to The Path Of Love and Yummy, which are completely sensible.

PART 3

HERVEY BAY/ FRASER ISLAND

There's an apartment block on the Gold Coast called Ohio. Someone obviously didn't get the memo when they were sending out guidelines for naming your building.

From the bus window you can see Maui Court, Bali Hai, Costa Dora, Montego Mermaid, Casa Del Torre, Outrigger Court, Pelican Sands...the names are meant to evoke something idyllic, something exotic, something holiday-ish.

But Ohio?

It's in the mid-west of the United States for god's sake. Admittedly, some of it does border a body of water, but that water belongs to Lake Erie, and apparently no one has ever uttered the words, 'I need a holiday where I can just sit on the beach, bliss out, get some sun and go swimming for a week—let's go to Ohio!'

Yes, I was back on the bus and, obviously, as I was noting down the names of apartment blocks, I was bored out of my mind. I was bored when we were in northern New South Wales, but then we crossed the border into Queensland, which made things just that little bit more boring. The bus radio was tuned to a station that seemed to be broadcasting from a wormhole in space, as the playlist included ABC's 'The Look of Love', John Waite's 'Missing You' and The Hooters' 'And We Danced'. That last one came out in 1985, which I think is the last time I heard it.

We passed through Currumbin, a town I recall from my childhood. As kids, we used to wear puffy parkas in winter, and a point of honour back in the 1970s was to have as many patches as possible plastered on the front and down the arms, representing different places around Australia. I remember buying a Currumbin patch, because this was the place that was the home of a bird sanctuary. We were all given tin plates of seed, and then hordes of parrots would descend on us, fluttering around our faces, landing on our heads, and pecking at the seed while our parents laughed their heads off and took photos. It was like a scene out of Hitchcock's *The Birds*.

From the bus window in 2007 I noticed that now it had become the Currumbin Wildlife Sanctuary—I guess birds alone are not such a big drawcard these days, so they needed to expand. Mind you, there's also a place called Honeyworld, which surely needs to sex up its image or broaden its appeal in order to get bodies through the door. Perhaps they should change the name to Condiment Universe and encapsulate jams, conserves and other spreads in order to reach a wider demographic.

Marketing didn't seem to be a strength in this part of the world. When we entered Palm Beach we were greeted by the following sign: WELCOME TO PALM BEACH—A WARM PLACE WITH WARM PEOPLE. A six-year-old must have spent absolute seconds coming up with that one.

I was also disturbed by the number of denture clinics I was seeing. Not dentists—denture clinics. Despite the protests of developers and resort owners that this was the vibrant, vital, happening future of the country, the sight of so many of these places really did bolster the old belief that the Gold Coast is where people go to die.

The girl sitting next to me suddenly asked what 'unapologetic aplomb' meant, a question I certainly wasn't expecting at that point. Or at any point on these travels, for that matter.

She wasn't doing a crossword, but reading the *Lonely Planet*, and had reached the section on Surfers Paradise. I leaned over to have a look where she was pointing on the page, and the normally staid publication certainly went into loquaciously critical overdrive in its summary, pointing out the city's 'constant commercial stimulus', adding that it achieved this with 'unapologetic aplomb', while warning travellers that once you enter the place, 'it's best to leave any delusions about discovering Australian culture behind'.

I tried to explain to her that they were saying Surfers Paradise was basically a hedonistic town that was overdeveloped, it was mainly about partying and having fun, and it was full of bars, nightclubs, theme parks and anything else that appealed to tourists, as long as it encouraged them to part with money.

'It's a great place to go if you want to get away from it all and relax,' I said.

'Really?' she asked, looking at me doubtfully.

'No,' I said. 'I'm being sarcastic.'

'Sorry, my English is not so great for me to understand sarcastic comments.'

Her name was Carla, and her English was actually very good. She was 20 years old and lived on a farm in Germany, an hour-and-a-half from Frankfurt. This was her first trip outside Europe, and so far she had only been to Melbourne and Canberra.

'You went to Canberra?' I asked. 'No one goes to Canberra.'

'Yes, I know this now,' she said.

She ended up sleeping on the streets for two nights, as she had brought very little spending money on the trip, and was sticking to a tight budget. It was encouraging to hear from someone who was actually travelling rough, but sleeping on the streets of Canberra was taking things a bit far. Carla was on her way to Noosa Heads, north of Brisbane, but asked more questions about Surfers Paradise, as every other backpacker she spoke to seemed to be stopping there, and she was wondering if she'd made a mistake by deciding to bypass it. So I told her about the Australian Rock Paper Scissors National Championships.

I had done some time in Surfers Paradise 18 months beforehand for a magazine story about this auspicious event.

Yes, there actually is a national contest dedicated to the art of throwing one of three signs with your hand. In fact, there's a global association and an extensive strategy guide that makes bewildering reading, not least because it is a 194 page book about a seemingly very simple children's game.

I stayed in a combined backpacker hostel/budget hotel with the other contestants, who had fashioned nicknames for themselves such as Spiderhands, Rock Steady, Split Seconds and Sideburns McGee, and descended on Surfers Paradise from all around the country. Wanting to get hands-on, I even entered the competition myself, choosing the intimidating stage name The Hand Of God. It wasn't intimidating enough because I was knocked out in my opening round, by a girl.

At the end of a hot, blustery, alcohol-soaked Sunday afternoon at the Fisherman's Wharf Tavern, a cavernous beer barn on the outskirts of town heaving with locals and tourists, one player finally emerged triumphant, a cool customer named Quinn 'The Doctor' Ramsden. He was a 24-year-old from Cairns who was studying psychology and psychotherapy. Maybe it was a mind game after all. As the winner, he got the chance to represent Australia in the world championships in Toronto later that year.

Back at the hotel, all the finalists were hanging out, swapping stories of the day's battles, surrounded by empty beer bottles, with the sweet smell of marijuana smoke drifting in from the balcony. The Doctor got to his feet to make a speech.

'I came here to hang out in Surfers, drink lots of beer, meet new people and have fun,' he said. 'And that's exactly what I've done. You're all champions.'

Everyone raised a toast to The Doctor, and wished him safe hands in Toronto. It was to no avail. He got over there and was knocked out in the first round. A man may be king of Surfers Paradise, but that doesn't mean a whole lot in the big bad world.

I explained to Carla that Surfers was a place where something as ridiculous as a Rock Paper Scissors National Championship kind of made sense. It was a place where a miniature golf course and a wax museum were still hanging in there, decades after these institutions died out in other parts of the country. It was a place that was the original and is still the number one destination for teenagers to get paralytic, carnal, aggressive and embarrassing during Schoolies Week. It was a place where women in gold bikinis, high heels and cowboy hats teetered around town putting money in parking meters. And it was a place where once a year the streets were transformed by seven temporary bridges, 2500 concrete barriers, 11,000 grandstand seats and over 25 kilometres of fencing, so a bunch of very loud, very fast cars could roar around a four-and-a-half kilometre track in a race called the Lexmark Indy 300.

'Now I wish I was maybe staying a few days there,' Carla said.

'Really?' I asked, wondering if she'd misunderstood me this whole time.

'No,' she said with a smile. 'Now *I* am being sarcastic.'

*   *   *

An hour later, the bus pulled into the station at Brisbane to pick up more passengers, and there he was, standing with his back and one foot up against a wall, casually smoking a cigarette, gazing off into the middle distance while a pretty girl with long brown hair was trying to engage him in conversation.

It was Dave, the Dutchman I'd met in Bondi, who had slept with five women in two weeks. I hadn't seen him for a week, so I guessed he must be into double figures by now.

Sure enough, he and the girl got on our bus, and sure enough they sat in the seat directly in front of mine. He looked at me and a flicker of recognition passed over his face, which I thought was pretty impressive considering I'm not female.

He introduced me to his new friend Iris, who was also from Holland. It turned out that he had bought a plane ticket from Sydney to Brisbane just half an hour before departure to join her here. Iris must have been some girl. They spent two days in Brisbane.

'You get the idea after one hour,' he said.

Within 10 minutes they fell asleep on each other.

As the bus crawled its way out of the city, I realised that this was the first time I'd ever travelled north of Brisbane in my life. I'd been to New York 12 times, but I'd never been to Maroochydore. I always thought this made me insufferably cosmopolitan, hip, and cool, three things that, even if they were true, were going to be of no use whatsoever where I was headed. This was my country, but the further I travelled, the more I felt like a tourist.

Carla got off the bus at Noosa Heads and told me she planned getting straight on another bus back to Surfers. She was really getting the hang of this sarcasm thing. Dave the Dutchman and his new girl said their goodbyes further up the coast at Rainbow Beach.

By this point my body felt like it had been dragged behind a truck for a kilometre, and no matter which way I positioned myself, even now that I had two seats to stretch out across, my ribcage really hurt. The day of surfing in Byron had obviously taken more out of me than I thought it did. Or maybe I was just older than I thought I was.

After unloading the backpacks for the Rainbow Beach stop, the driver started the engine again, and in a haze of tiredness, I looked out the window as Dave gave a small wave, and smiled with a cigarette clamped between his lips. I waved back and wondered if he was feeling anything more for the girl he was with than he had for all the other easy liaisons he'd had back in Bondi. I watched as the two of them walked away, and I noticed his left hand drop and search for her hand. Then the bus pulled away and I lost sight of them.

This little ant had to ride the dog a little longer to get further north to Hervey Bay.

*　　*　　*

'Sadly, yes. More than enough.'

That's the answer I got from the girl at the hostel reception in response to the question: 'Will one day in Hervey Bay be long enough to see everything it has to offer?'

Apparently Hervey Bay has one of the three best climates on earth. The average temperature is 23°C...in winter. The average in summer is 30°C. But as you may suspect from a town whose major claim to fame is its weather, it's not the most happening place on the planet.

In fact, it's a favoured destination for retirees and those seeking a seachange later in life. In the last 30 years, these people have swelled the population from 8000 to 52,000. It's not a huge town, but it's spread out and dotted with homes that look like holiday houses on nicely manicured lawns. Over 600,000 tourists come through every year, but the overwhelming reason they're here is because this is the major stepping-off point to get to Fraser Island. Indeed, that's why I was here.

A strange thing happened in Hervey Bay. The minute I got off the bus, I fell into a funk. I seemed to have a sign above my head that flashed different messages, the most popular being 'ignore me', 'patronise me', 'have nothing to do with me' and 'shit me to tears'. There was a shuttle bus to Koala's, the backpacker hostel where I was going to be staying, and the driver introduced himself as our 'chauffeur and barman' and made lots of bad, but good-natured jokes.

'Hervey Bay has a lot to offer,' he said. 'I know it may not look like it, but really, it does. Ask me anything you like about the place. Go on. Anything.'

Silence. Everyone studied their shoes. It was a little embarrassing.

So I gave it a go.

'Where can I find a good coffee around here. I haven't had one since Sydney.'

Tumbleweeds rolled past. A cricket chirped. Someone coughed.

'Well, I don't drink coffee myself,' our driver finally said. 'But there's a café about 7 minutes walk to the left of the hostel. The woman there used to make a good iced coffee, but I'm not sure if she's still working there. Or if she's still alive.'

We got to Koala's, which sat on a strip of road that hugged the bay, and there were two receptionists on duty at the office. I was first off the bus and walked over to the girl who wasn't already dealing with a customer. She chewed gum frantically and stared at a computer screen. I stood there and waited. And waited. And waited. And waited.

She didn't look up. From behind her another backpacker stood up from one of the internet computers and approached a counter to her right. She immediately went over to help him.

I looked around for a mirror to see if I actually existed. Perhaps I had become Bruce Willis in *The Sixth Sense*. A new receptionist arrived at the next station and five people from the bus immediately lined up there, right next to where I was standing. I stared at the new receptionist with what I hoped was my best look of disbelief on my face. Couldn't she see I was standing there and being ignored?

'You'll have to go the back of this line, mate. No one can help you standin' there. It's not a line.'

'Well, it was a line, actually,' I said in my head. 'There was actually a gormless, rude imbecile who could have been helpin' me about 30 seconds ago but she ignored me and chewed gum like a cow and now she's standin' over there helpin' someone else even though I was here before them, and can't you see all of this, you stupid bitch?'

But I just glumly picked up my backpack and trudged to the end of the line like an errant schoolboy, my fellow passengers giving me vaguely accusatory looks, as if I was trying to push in or something.

Half an hour later—and that's not an exaggeration—it really was 30 minutes later, I finally got to the head of the line. The person before me was literally standing there for 15 minutes in animated discussion with the receptionist, who patiently answered all her questions and showed her brochures and made suggestions and drew out a little map for her so she could find her room in the complex.

Well, I thought to myself, at least the wait will be worth it as they seemed so thorough.

'Okay mate, I'm about to finish my shift, so let's get moving,' she said.

I paid for the night, she thrust a key into my hand, pointed vaguely in the direction of where I'd find my room and got up from her seat.

'Um, don't I need a sheet for the bed?' I asked.

'Oh, yeah. Hang on.'

She disappeared and grudgingly returned with one.

'Um, can I ask you some questions about trips to Fraser Island?'

'Mate, they're basically all the same.'

'Well, I heard there are self-drive tours and organised tours and you can stay two or three days.'

'Yeah, yeah. But you know, whatever. Here's a couple of brochures. Just have a look at them tonight and come back tomorrow.'

'But I want to go to Fraser Island tomorrow, so I'll need to book it tonight.'

'Mate, I was meant to be finished half an hour ago, so I gotta go.'

How helpful. And I really wished she would stop calling me 'mate'.

I wandered through the grounds of the hostel, which looked like a motel complex, complete with kidney-shaped swimming pool. Night had fallen, and I took 10 minutes to find my room.

I opened the door, found an empty bed among the familiar four double-decker bunks, and got talking to two of my room-mates. One was from Korea and his name was Woojin, but he told me to call him Ad. I had no idea why. He seemed nice enough, but his grasp of English was about as tight as my grasp on my sanity at that moment, so communication was difficult.

Lying on the bed opposite was the straightest, dullest French-Canadian I have ever met—if you have ever met any

French-Canadians, you will realise this is really saying something.

I said I was going to the bar to get a beer if they'd like to join me, but Woojin/Ad was cooking with his friends, and the French-Canadian said he 'must look through these brochures now', pointing to a stack of colour booklets next to his bed.

I walked down to the bar, drank two beers in quick succession, ate some pasta, then called my friend Kathy in Sydney and moaned like a small, irritating child about the fact I couldn't get people to like me and my story was vanishing down a black hole from which it would never return. And my ribs hurt. She made encouraging noises and told me things would get better.

I had trouble sleeping that night. The general aches, pains, bruises and scrapes from my day of surfing had started to settle down a little, which only accentuated the fact that there was a constant sharp pain in my right side, like someone was pushing a knife in and then slowly twisting it. The next morning it was so bad that I visited a doctor, who informed me that it looked very much like I'd got a cracked rib.

'Have you done anything recently that would have caused that?'

'Two days ago I spent six hours learning to surf, with the board bashing against my ribcage a lot of the time,' I said.

'Well, that would probably do it,' she said with a smile.

She also told me that apart from taking pain relief medication there was absolutely nothing I could do about it apart from waiting for it to heal.

'Roughly how long will that take?' I asked.

'Could be up to six or eight weeks,' she told me. 'It'll help if you avoid any bumping or jolting or strenuous physical activity for a while.'

Two hours later I was on Fraser Island, where I spent the next three days in a four-wheel drive vehicle that traversed unpredictable, rutted sandy tracks with all the grace of a drunk wallaby. Every 10 minutes we would hit a bump so big that I left my seat and my head almost hit the roof. And then I'd come down again. I'd grimace and hold my right side tightly, imagining the crack in my rib widening, then splitting, and the ragged edges piercing through my chest. This probably wasn't what the good doctor had in mind.

Sorry, I'm going on a bit here. You don't want to hear me whinge and whine and blow things out of proportion, even if, honestly, please believe me, I was in real pain. But as I was on my way to Fraser Island, it's kind of appropriate to maybe—just maybe—get a bit melodramatic. It's what Eliza Fraser, after whom the island is named, would have done.

Mrs Fraser got to the island 171 years before me, but apparently she endured more than a cracked rib. She was travelling from Sydney to Singapore on a boat called the *Stirling Castle*, which was under the command of her husband, Captain James Fraser.

The boat struck a reef in May 1836, and those on board had to scramble aboard two lifeboats that were in dubious condition. They ended up landing on the island and...well, at this point let me type out the title of the book Eliza wrote and published about her experiences: *Narrative of the capture, sufferings, and miraculous escape of Mrs. Eliza Fraser, wife of the late Captain James Fraser commander of the ship Stirling Castle which was wrecked on 25th May, in latitude 34, and longitude 155, 12, east, on Eliza Reef, on her passage from New South Wales to Liverpool-a part of the crew having taken to the long boat, were driven to and thrown on an unknown island, inhabited by Savages, by whom Captain Fraser and his first mate were barbarously murdered, and Mrs. Fraser (the wife of the former, with the 2d mate and steward, were for several weeks held in bondage) and after having been compelled to take up her abode in a wigwam and to become the adopted wife of one of the Chiefs, Mrs F. was providentially rescued from her perilous situation.*

Snappy title, yes? Apparently (a) Eliza wasn't the most succinct of writers, and (b) marketing people with an eye for a catchy title weren't so thick on the ground in publishing circles back then.

Renowned eccentric singer-songwriter Fiona Apple suddenly looks like the soul of brevity for calling her 1999 album *When the Pawn Hits the Conflicts He Thinks like a King What He Knows Throws the Blows When He Goes to the Fight and He'll Win the Whole Thing 'Fore He Enters the Ring There's No Body to Batter When Your Mind Is Your Might So When You Go Solo, You Hold Your Own Hand and Remember That Depth Is the Greatest of Heights and If*

You Know Where You Stand, Then You Know Where to Land and If You Fall It Won't Matter, 'Cuz You'll Know That You're Right.

Mrs Fraser's book became a bestseller back in England, which is remarkable when you consider that not only would no one be able to ask for it by name, but the entire story was there on the cover anyway.

It turns out that Eliza was perhaps not the most reliable of narrators. Over the years her story changed considerably (and wildly) in the telling. Doubts have been cast on her accounts of the brutal behaviour of the Aborigines, and about her claim that her husband died in her arms as the result of a spear injury (others say that the Captain was in bad health anyway and actually died of starvation).

Also, an escaped convict named David Bracewell, who it was rumoured helped Eliza escape and get to safety, was not only wiped from her history of events, but she threatened to dob him in to the authorities, causing him to go on the run. Even the cause of her death a couple of decades later is not clear—it was reported that she was killed in a road accident in 1858, but other accounts claim she became mentally unstable and died in an institution.

Unsurprisingly, her story has captured the imagination over the years, being the basis of novels by Patrick White and Michael Ondaatje, a series of paintings by Sidney Nolan, and the 1976 film *Eliza Fraser*, starring Susannah York.

Of course, the Aboriginal people got here a little before both myself and Eliza Fraser. About 5000 years before. The

Butchulla people named the island K'gari. The legend said that the god Beeral sent the goddess K'gari down to earth to create the mountains, the sea and the rivers. K'gari ended up loving the place so much that she didn't want to leave, so she was turned into a beautiful island so she could stay forever.

When you first see Fraser Island, even from the comfort of a high-speed ferry in the first part of the early 21st century, it's easy to see how it could provide the backdrop for such tales. It's a remarkable looking place. There is, quite literally, sand everywhere. It's over 120 kilometres long, and between 5 and 15 kilometres wide, making it the largest sand island on earth. The only way to get around is on tricky tracks that wind and undulate around the island, and the only way to traverse these is in a four-wheel drive vehicle.

The lone traveller can do this two ways. One is to get seven or eight or nine people together, hire a small vehicle, stock up on supplies (mainly alcohol) and go for it for three days. At first I thought I'd go for this option, but as well as hearing stories that this was a great way to get really drunk with strangers rather than actually see much of the island, the decision was made for me. There were no available spots the next day, and I didn't feel like hanging around Hervey Bay for longer than 24 hours.

I decided to join a small tour group of around 30 backpackers on a four-wheel drive bus with a driver/guide. I'm not normally one for organised tours or moving from place to place with a gaggle of people, but as I was starting to feel like a tourist, it felt like the right time to really become one for a few days.

My decision was vindicated the next day when we passed a four-wheel drive that was resting quite comfortably on its roof. The driver was still inside, laughing. His passengers were sitting on the sand and they were not laughing. In fact, they looked pretty pissed off.

When we got to the island after a 30-minute crossing, we were introduced to Matt, our driver. He was a Buddha-shaped bloke with a red face, short-cropped grey hair, squinty eyes and a mischievous grin. We found out later that he'd only been doing the job for a couple of months, which would explain his inability to answer any questions that were more probing than 'When's lunch?' He had the bad stage patter down, mainly consisting of cheap innuendo involving alcohol consumption and sex stereotypes.

'If we get bogged in the sand, you girls can get out and push,' he said more than once, leaving one of his trademark pauses that went just a little too long. 'And you guys can take photos.'

He also had a stock of comments for when the bus hit a particularly large bump in the road, making everyone airborne for a few seconds. These included the immortal 'Still awake up the back?' and old favourite 'It's the most fun you can have with your clothes on'.

But as for any vaguely probing questions relating to the island itself, whether it was the geography, history or wildlife, Matt only had a 50 per cent strike rate. At one point, while we were hiking around on a headland looking for a landmark called the Champagne Pools, I got the distinct impression he didn't know where he was going, and the look of relief on his face when we finally found the right way was palpable. Fortunately he knew how to drive like a demon, unlike our friends in the overturned vehicle, and for that we had to be thankful.

Matt drove us up the hill from the jetty and we dumped our gear at our lodgings, a place called the Kingfisher Bay Resort. I know the word 'resort' sounds luxurious, but let me point out that although we weren't staying in tents, there was no jacuzzi, maid service or daily massages. And the girls who were staying in a room next to mine had to be moved because there were bedbugs all through their sheets. Still, it was pleasant hostel accommodation, with just four people to each cabin-like room, fitted out with two double-decker bunks and a balcony.

Then we hit the road. Or rather, we hit the sand.

The name Kingfisher Bay Resort sounded vaguely familiar, but it wasn't until we were back in the bus and crossing the electrified grid connected to the perimeter fence that I remembered why. Back in 2004, two parents who were staying here with their kids woke to the sound of their five-year-old screaming. When they got into the room, they saw their daughter standing in front of the bed where the couple's three-month-old baby was sleeping. Between the two children was a dingo.

The parents scared the animal away, and no one was hurt, but three years previously, a nine-year-old was mauled to death. They estimate there are between 100 and 200 dingoes on the island. Although I didn't want to wake up in the middle of the night with the hot breath of a dingo on my face, I was looking forward to seeing one from a safe distance sometime over the next two nights and three days.

We'd been swimming for around 15 minutes and were still only halfway across Lake McKenzie when Jeff told me that he had been part of the NATO peacekeeping force in Kosovo in 1999.

He was a wiry English guy with glasses and a nervy smile. When he suggested we try to make it across the lake, I figured that if he was up for it, then I was up for it too. But— and I promise this is the third last time I'll mention this—I had that cracked rib to contend with.

And then, with the same length of water ahead of us as there was behind, and with both of us encouraging each other to keep going even though we were flagging, he told me that eight years ago he celebrated his 21st birthday while he was serving in Kosovo.

'At the time, I hated it,' he admitted. 'I thought I was just a glorified policeman, trying to stop people from killing each other. But it was a good experience in retrospect.'

Jesus. When I turned 21 I had a party in my parents' backyard and my major concern was hiring a jukebox with cool songs on it. This guy was so hardy he could probably swim to Sydney. He was in a war zone at an age when I was stumbling through university. And he was modest about it, too. I grilled him about his time there, and he casually mentioned that he was given a medal for his service. I made 'I'm impressed' noises.

'Mate, it's nothing. Really. Everyone gets one. It's basically saying, "Thanks very much for being here".'

He counted himself lucky. One friend of his was killed in Afghanistan and two others were injured by a suicide bomber.

It took us another 20 minutes to get to the other side, where we gave each other high-fives, and then reclined there in the shallows hoping that our heart rates would return to normal and those black spots in front of our eyes would soon fade. I was heartened to see that he appeared as out of breath as I was.

It looked like a scene out of the movie *The Beach*. Here we were in the middle of the forest in the middle of an island in the middle of the ocean, a hundred metres above sea level, and there were 150 hectares of water around us, ringed by pure white sand, then thick bush. The reason lakes can form here is because compacted sand and decomposing vegetable matter effectively create a shell to contain the water, turning the area into a giant natural swimming pool.

As we took in the scene, Jeff told me about his travels. He came from Devon in the United Kingdom and drove trucks for a living. He'd been on the road for the last 16 months. He spent a month catching buses across the United States, then spent two weeks in Fiji, before getting to New Zealand and finding work on an orchard at Motueka in the south island. He liked New Zealand so much that he stayed from November 2005 to July 2006, and then came to Australia, where he spent almost six months working on a farm on King Island, the windblown dot on the map off Tasmania that's famous for its cheese and dairy products.

Jeff was unlike anyone I had met on my travels. He liked a drink and liked to party, but he seemed to truly enjoy his own company, and genuinely loved working. He said that he hankered to do something with his hands and learn about the country and the people rather than fritter away his time.

'That time in New Zealand was when I really settled into life as a traveller,' he said. 'And on King Island I fell in love with the farm as soon as I got here. The work was hard and the hours were long and there was a lot of cow shit, but I was learning so much, and I just found this really happy balance between work and friends and life.'

We'd been lying there in the water for a while and decided there was no way we were swimming back, so started walking around the edge of the lake in the blazing sun. We started talking about women, as two men who have bonded over a long swim will.

It turned out that Jeff didn't have a lot of luck with the ladies. When he told me that he and his army buddies would basically wander around a club towards closing time and ask every woman in the place straight-up if they fancied a shag, I began to see how his approach may have needed a bit of re-tooling.

'You'd be surprised,' he told me. 'If you don't mind asking a lot and getting a lot of rejections, one will eventually say yes. I'm not saying she'll be attractive, but still.'

He alluded to the fact that before he left England, he was criminally shy. I must admit that he did seem a little jittery and eager to please, but I'd warmed to him from the moment we met in the line to board the boat to Fraser Island.

He lamented the fact that although he'd made some good friends while travelling, he'd only had sex with one girl in that time, and was hoping to change that. I told him that the method he'd just outlined possibly wasn't the way to go. Although, thinking about what I'd seen thus far, at three a.m. in a pub full of backpackers, it was possibly exactly the way to go. I decided it was my mission to turn Jeff into a lean, mean, lady-loving machine.

And anyone who read that last sentence and knows me even slightly—after wiping the tears of mirth from their eyes—will now be thinking that this is a case of the blind leading the blind. Still, over the previous 18 months, I'd written a few stories on modern dating and relationships, and come across Neil Strauss's book *The Game*. Strauss was a bald, skinny, geeky music journalist, so we were kind of on the same page. He researched and wrote a story on the world of professional pick-up artists, and then became so engrossed in it that he set up house with them, infiltrating their world and learning all their tricks. In the process, the apprentice became the master, and he wrote a very entertaining book about the subject.

I told Jeff about some of the basic stuff he wrote about, and how, like that episode of *Seinfeld* where George did the opposite of everything he'd ever learned, sometimes we had to invert our behaviour and go against our instincts to get results. I told him about negging (a light-hearted criticism that's designed to get a reaction) and being cocky and funny, even if it doesn't come naturally to you.

Jeff had never heard anything like this before and started peppering me with questions. When we finally got back to the rest of the group on the other side of the lake, and then returned to the bus, he made me write down the name of the book and the author, and vowed to buy it at the next available opportunity. Two young Swiss girls were sitting in the seats next to us. I'm not sure if it was my imagination, but as Jeff struck up a conversation with them, I swear he seemed to be a little more confident than he'd been before our swim.

The first night on the island, after we got back to our rooms and had showered, I was sitting on the balcony looking out at the bush and writing in my notebook, when Tom flopped down next to me and told me all about himself. Tom was like a long-lost Kray brother. He came from south London, and he looked, spoke and acted like a crim on *The Bill*. He flew into Sydney three weeks ago, his mates met him at the airport, and the only thing he remembers of the next three days is that he definitely didn't sleep once.

'We got on the piss and then we started doin' pills.'

What kind of pills?

'E's,' he said. 'E's and then sniff.'

That's ecstasy and cocaine for my more sheltered readers.

'It's expensive 'ere though, innit? Quality's good though. E's at 'ome are nothin' now. They're givin' em away. The quality ain't as good. They've flooded the market, 'aven't they?'

I suppose they 'ave. Over the next two nights, I noticed Tom disappear every now and then to the bathroom and then re-appear considerably refreshed, rubbing his nose, with his eyes wide and darting. It seemed like he was sorted for sniff, then, even if he wasn't offering it around.

He told me that in Bondi, he'd lived in a two-bedroom flat with eight people. Over three weeks he saw a bit of Darling Harbour and the city, but mainly he saw the inside of clubs and the inside of his flat. There were cockroaches and spiders everywhere in that place, and the housemates had a rule that they wouldn't kill any of them. Not immediately, anyway. Instead they had to put an overturned glass on top of any insect they found. The whole place was like some bizarre museum, littered with glasses that housed creatures that were either dying or decomposing. It was like sharing a house with Crispin Glover and Marilyn Manson.

Plop! Smash!

There goes another one.

'Whoops!' said someone.

Plop! Smash!

There goes another one. A hand goes up to cover a mouth.

It was one in the morning and everyone was crammed onto the balcony attached to the room where 'the English dudes with the guitars' were staying.

The English dudes with the guitars were from south London and they used to be in a band together. Mark, on one guitar, was their cheeky leader. Ed, on the other guitar, was the tall, skinny, quiet one. Brad was the swaggering, jovial, drunk singer. And Chris, the joker with the pierced lip and the goofy laugh, was the equivalent of Bez in Happy Mondays, or that bloke who used to dance and shout a lot in Madness. He was half-mascot, half-performing monkey. He also seemed to be some sort of vaudevillian, cranking out quips and one-liners as if he was performing in a hotel in some faded English seaside town.

'Where you from?' he'd asked another English guy on our bus earlier in the day.

'Portsmouth,' he'd replied.

'Portsmouth's like my front room,' said Chris, pausing for a beat. 'Nothing in it.'

Plop! Smash!

And another beer bottle went over the edge of the balcony, landing on the footpath below.

A call went up for the Counting Crows' 'Mr Jones'. Mark and Ed struck the opening chords together without even consulting each other, Brad sang the first verse without even taking his cigarette out of his mouth, and Chris broke off from his ska-inspired dancing to provide a falsetto harmony in the chorus.

Plop! Smash!

There goes another one.

They say that all the sand on the east coast of Australia eventually comes to rest on Fraser Island. And if the amount that ended up in my Speedos and shoes is any indication, then I believe it. The stuff is everywhere. The island is basically a giant sandbar with trees and lakes on it.

The next morning I found myself at the top of the most dramatic piece of sand on the island, a dune that was 50 metres high. It was so impressive that you could have filmed a *Star Wars* sequel there. It wasn't exactly vertical, but as I was lying on a boogie board ready to surrender my body to gravity, and the base of the dune abruptly ended in a pool of water known as Lake Wabby, it may as well have been. Did I also mention that I had a cracked rib? Okay, just checking.

I let go, my left hand gripping the board, my right hand clutching my ribcage. The board built up speed rapidly and frantically bumped along the sand, before hitting the water, throwing me into a somersault as I slapped the surface. The second time I tried it standing up. The third time I actually succeeded in doing the whole thing standing up.

There was a good reason we were doing all our swimming in the islands' lakes. You *can* swim in the water off Fraser Island. Let me add something to that sentence—you *can* swim in the water off Fraser Island, if you want to risk being drowned as a result of being caught in one of the notorious rips, or being eaten by one of the many sharks that negotiate those notorious rips with a lot more skill than the average backpacker.

Matt had dropped us at Lake Wabby and left us with instructions to hang out for a while, exhaust ourselves by sledding down the dune and acting like idiots, then climb the long, steep dune to the east, keep following the marked trail through the bush for around 40 minutes, and eventually we'd get to the ocean on the other side, where he'd be waiting in the bus with his feet up and a cool drink in his hand.

'And keep your eyes out for dingoes!' he called out as he got back in the bus. We still hadn't spotted one.

He left, and it immediately started to rain in big, fat drops, but then passed half an hour later, just in time for the sun to make a blazing return to form for our long uphill trek on soft sand.

After a headcount on the other side, Matt steered the bus out onto the beach and let it rip. The beach here operates like a primitive highway with its own set of road rules, where buses have right of way over self-driven four-wheel drives. There's only one thing the buses don't have right of way over, and that's aircraft. Yes, a stretch of the beach is also a runway for sightseeing planes.

We made a couple of stops along the way—one to float down Eli Creek, a cool, shallow freshwater stream that winds its way down through the forest to the beach. And later we paused to check out the wreck of the *Maheno*, a ship which was being towed to Japan to be broken up for scrap in 1935. It didn't get very far, as a cyclone hit the northern Queensland coast, and the *Maheno* washed up here, where it has sat ever since, a rusting skeleton encrusted with barnacles. It was used for target practice for fighter planes during WWII, and the fact that it survives over 60 years later is a testament to either the superb shipbuilding skills of the day, or the poor shooting skills of the day. Jeff and I took turns posing for photos with the Swiss girls, Sabrina and Martina, standing at the front of the wreck and imitating Leonardo DiCaprio and Kate Winslet in *Titanic* while singing terrible renditions of 'My Heart Will Go On'.

Back on the bus we rattled along further north, and the cliffs to our left, which are called The Pinnacles, showed off seams of compacted sand in a rainbow of colours, from dusky reds to burnt oranges and bright yellows. And at the end of the beach we finally reached an impressive mass of rock called Indian Head that juts out into the ocean. After a long, hot 30-minute climb to the top, we looked down to see stingrays dotting the water below, and then descended to wallow in the only bit of salt water where you could safely swim on the island. The Champagne Pools were created by natural rock formations facing the ocean and with every incoming wave, the warm, shallow water churned and bubbled. It was like nature's jacuzzi and we all luxuriated in it for ages with stupid smiles on our faces.

*　　*　　*

'The Contiki tour is on the island tonight,' Matt told us on the bus trip back to the resort at the end of the day. 'And you know what that means.'

Apparently that means a lot of people getting very drunk while dressed up as something beginning with the letter 'S'. Subsequently, we watched a passing parade of costumes as we sat in the bar—sailors, sex workers (or possibly sluts?), a nun (who I guess was meant to be a sister), a very buxom and unchaste looking Snow White, and a bunch of people dressed as South Koreans, which wasn't really too imaginative, as they actually were South Koreans.

At one in the morning, I watched Snow White and mother superior have a very drunk, very heated discussion, apparently about a guy dressed as Sinbad, who was taking the first syllable of his name to heart and cheating on his girlfriend. Snow White used language which I don't recall hearing in the Disney movie. Bashful would not have been the only dwarf to blush at her comments.

As was the case in many night-time establishments frequented by backpackers, the management seemed to think that their patrons were incapable of getting legless all by themselves, so they kindly assisted them in this. And as was also the case in many night-time establishments frequented by backpackers, the organiser was a girl who screamed like a banshee into the microphone.

'Aaaaaaaalriiiiiiiiiiiight!' she howled. 'You people need to have a good time! So it's time for boat races! Teams of five! Come on! You know you want to!'

I could see no boats, and we weren't near any water at that moment, so I wondered what form these boat races would take. The English musicians in our group—Mark, Brad, Ed and Chris—had gatecrashed the fancy dress party by swathing themselves in sheets that they'd taken from their beds, and they teamed up with a Swedish girl they'd befriended, and entered the competition.

It worked like this: two teams of five stood on a raised platform with beers lined up in front of them. The first four had pots; the last had a pint. At the signal from the screaming banshee, the first player in each team would chug down the beer and then upturn the empty glass on their head, which was the signal for the next person in their team to do the same.

This went on until the end, when the team whose pint-drinker finished first was the winner of that round. At the end of each round there was much backslapping and high-fiving, as if this was the greatest sporting achievement anyone had seen since the last Olympics. It also meant that everyone got quite drunk quite quickly.

Up to this point I'd been astounded by the south London guys' ability to consume so much alcohol and still function the next day. I was even more astounded—as they were—to find that they were knocked out in the very first round. Those Contiki groups are a tough breed.

It was two a.m., and I was dancing to the Scissor Sisters' 'I Don't Feel Like Dancing'. Again.

As we were in the middle of a dance floor in the middle of a wilderness area, it all seemed very incongruous at first. But at a certain point your backpacker brain takes over and gradually it didn't seem so strange. Everyone was happy and tipsy. I was dancing with Sabrina and Martina, whose combined ages did not reach my own, but who had seemed to have adopted me as some sort of eccentric but basically harmless uncle. We invented ridiculous dances such as the shampoo, the shopping trolley, and, my personal favourite, big fish, little fish, cardboard box.

Every time I was with a group of people and 'I Don't Feel Like Dancing' came on, everyone felt like dancing, making it possibly the most ironically named song in pop music history. The song became the track of the summer, and you heard it in shops, all across the radio dial, and in every pub and club for weeks and weeks.

At the end of the trip I calculated that I must have danced to 'I Don't Feel Like Dancing' five times a week for a month, and I heard it many more times than that when not in the vicinity of a dance floor. The Scissor Sisters were providing the theme tune to this whole exercise, and it made me think about music and travelling.

I can't hear The Triffids' 'Wide Open Road' without thinking of my friend Frank, as it's the song we used to sing to ourselves when we were hitch-hiking together in England and Wales 20 years ago.

The entire R.E.M. album *Life's Rich Pageant* will always evoke memories of Kyle, an American guy I met on a train in

Italy in 1986, who loaned me the cassette tape just before he boarded a ferry to Greece. I was taking a later boat, but he entrusted me with what was then the band's brand new album, and said he'd see me on the other side. We ended up travelling together and becoming long-time friends, all stemming from a love of the same band.

In 1991, I was travelling around the United States, and in a record store in Austin, Texas a song came over the speakers that sounded so incredible it made me stop flicking through the racks. I had no idea what it was. The guitars sounded massive, the drums thundered, the tune was so undeniably great that I couldn't believe no one had come up with it before, and the guy kept singing yeah-yeah-yeah-yeah over and over again, sounding like he was on the edge of completely shredding his voice. I went up to the counter and asked what it was.

'It's Nirvana,' the guy told me. 'They're from Seattle. They're gonna be huge.'

I bought the cassette of the *Nevermind* album, which had just come out that week, and along with The Pixies' *Trompe Le Monde,* it became the soundtrack of the rest of my trip.

Not all my musical signposts are insufferably cool. I always associate Kim Wilde's anodyne cover of 'You Keep Me Hanging On' with the lowest paid job I have ever had, working as a waiter in a restaurant in Wimbledon. It seemed to come on the radio every hour, along with Simply Red's 'Holding Back The Years', and whenever I have the misfortune to hear these two songs today, they inevitably take me back to my twenty-something self, eking out an English winter in a ridiculous blue waiter's coat, earning one pound and 70 pence an hour.

When I was in my twenties, the Walkman was the only way to take music with you when you were on the road, so compilation cassettes often provided the accompaniment to plane rides and bus trips and train journeys. The tapes would wear thin from repeated plays, and the order of the songs would be forever imprinted on my brain—The Go-Betweens' 'Bachelor Kisses' followed by The Modern Lovers' 'Someone I Care About' followed by R.E.M.'s 'Driver 8' followed by Elvis Costello's 'I Can't Stand Up For Falling Down' followed by The Smiths' 'This Charming Man' followed by Lloyd Cole And The Commotions' 'Forest Fire', and on and on, a list of songs that became so entrenched in that order that for years afterwards I would hear one of those songs in isolation and when it ended, I'd expect the next song from that mix tape to kick in.

The nature of travel soundtracking has changed now. With iPods, backpackers can take hundreds of songs around with them, hit the scrolling wheel to decide what they want and when they want it, or listen to everything on random shuffle, or rip music from fellow travellers' devices and refresh their collections daily. You no longer have to rely on the small number of 90-minute cassettes you can squeeze in your backpack or on a wallet crammed with CDs.

But at the same time, the songs that make up the memories of your trip are now more diffuse, spread across four or eight or 30 or 80 gigabytes. There are a lot more songs, but perhaps individual ones don't have the same strong association with certain places, certain people and certain events.

Today when I hear those first heartbeat thumps of 'Wide Open Road', I'm back standing with Frank in the gravel on a Welsh roadside, hoping for a ride to the next town. I wonder if in 20 years time, when some oldies station plays a 'Commercial-Free Noughties Pop Block' and 'I Don't Feel Like Dancing' comes on, my mind will immediately spin back to that time I backpacked up the east coast of Australia for a month in 2007?

I'll get back to you on that.

'We may not have seen any dingoes on this trip,' Matt said over the microphone as we set out on the bus for our last day on Fraser. 'But what about koalas? Scientists say there are no koalas on the island, but I've been told that a couple have been sighted recently, so keep your eyes peeled.'

The last couple of days had developed their own rhythm. The bus would rattle over bumpy sand tracks for an hour or so, we'd stop to go for a walk through lush bush and occasionally come across some wildlife (goannas, frogs, flies, no dingoes), and then come across a pristine lake, where we would swim, laze about on the sand, and play torrid games of beach cricket involving the UK versus the rest of the world. On the last morning we went for one final bush walk and ended up at Lake Birrabeen, where everyone promptly splashed in the shallows and then flaked out in the blazing sun. A couple of days of this not-so-frantic activity had taken its toll, and we were weary and ready to move back to the mainland.

On the bus trip back to the wharf for the trip home on the boat, Matt got back on the microphone.

'If you look out the left hand side of the bus folks, I think we might be able to see one of those koalas I was telling you about.'

We looked, and there was a toy koala hanging limply in a tree. There were collective groans. Then Matt hit the accelerator again, we hit a big pothole, and everyone became airborne again.

'Still awake up the back?' said Matt, thankfully for the final time on the trip.

When I got back to Koala's in Hervey Bay, I was exhausted. I was allocated a new room, and when I found it, there were three guys sitting on the porch with a bunch of beers. I said hello and they grunted. I persisted, and their spokesman, an English guy with a thick northern accent, perked up a little. He told me about the Swedish girl in our room.

'I can't even talk to her she's so beautiful,' he said, with surprising tenderness for a guy with a shaved head and multiple tatts, holding a beer and a cigarette.

All three of them kept looking up at the sky, which was starting to grow dark.

'We're waiting for the bats,' explained the English guy. 'Have you seen the bats here before?'

I hadn't.

'Just you wait. It's amazing. They fly over here at dusk. Hundreds of 'em. Of all the Australian animals I've seen, they're my favourite. They just look perfect against the sky.'

He was strangely poetic for a guy who looked like he could beat you over the head with a pool cue for no reason whatsoever.

Ten minutes later the bats started making their way overhead, first only a few, then dozens, then the air was thick with them, their wings making that perfect Batman-shaped insignia against the darkening sky. All four of us were silent for minutes on end as they passed over.

'Amazing, innit?' the English guy finally said, in a hushed voice. And it really was. He had a smile of wonder on his face that made him look like a six-year-old kid. And then I realised that I was smiling too.

After the bats had finished their flyover, I went inside, had a shower, and when I walked out to the balcony to hang out my towel, the guys were gone. But when I turned back to enter the room I realised someone was sitting there on the bench. Somehow I knew this had to be the Swedish girl. She really was beautiful. And I wasn't wearing a shirt. Now, I'm not the kind of guy who takes off his shirt to make himself more attractive, and even though it was quite dark, this was an awkward moment. I said hi, and then realised she was wearing iPod headphones, but she took them out and engaged me in conversation, so I just stood there with my shirt off.

Her name was Anna, she'd been travelling for two months, and she was heading to Fraser Island tomorrow, so I told her about my trip. I asked to have a look at her iPod and gave her some light-hearted ribbing about having Nickelback on there. After 15 minutes she said she was heading off to meet some friends at Morocco's, the nightclub attached to the hostel, and that I should come down and meet up for a drink later.

It must have been darker than I thought.

I'd walked past Morocco's the night I'd first got to Hervey Bay. I could see through a half-open door that there were only about half a dozen people inside, and although there was absolutely no one lining up outside to get in, there were two bouncers on the door.

'Coming in tonight, bro?' one of them asked me.

'Maybe later,' I said. 'I'd have to get changed first, anyway.'

I was wearing shorts and thongs at the time.

'No problem, mate,' said the other bouncer. 'We'll let you in like that.'

Business appeared to be so slow at Morocco's that these bouncers had become anti-bouncers, inhabiting some topsy-turvy world where they'd come up with any excuse to get people inside rather than the usual practice of coming up with any excuse to keep them waiting outside.

I said goodbye to Anna, went back inside and lay down on the bed, thinking I'd just rest my eyes, and then head down there in half an hour or so. I woke up three hours later to the sound of Anna and her friends coming back. It was one in the morning.

'You didn't miss anything,' Anna told me. 'There were about 12 people there, all standing around looking at each other. And the music was terrible. We had some free drink tickets, and that's the only reason we stayed there for this long.'

As I drifted back to sleep I heard her put her iPod on as she got into the bunk opposite me. The faint bouncy piano and distinctive beat sounded familiar. Sure enough, it was 'I Don't Feel Like Dancing'.

The following morning I wandered around Hervey Bay to see how long I could stretch out its delights. About an hour, as it turned out.

I went for a swim at the 'beach', which was actually a long, thin strip of sand facing the bay. Astoundingly, there was a lifeguard on duty. The 'waves' were basically ripples that you could measure in centimetres, not metres. The guy was about 19, he had his own beach buggy, and he sat in a folding deckchair with a drink in his hand. I'm not sure how he secured this job, but I'd hazard a guess that he had pictures of Hervey Bay's mayor in a compromising position with a donkey.

'Do the waves ever get any bigger than this?' I asked him.

'This is about it,' he replied.

'Had to save anyone lately?'

He looked at me warily, like I might be taking the piss, or had a hidden camera.

'Not lately, no,' he said cautiously. Perhaps not wanting to encourage any further questions from this inquisitive beach-goer, he returned his gaze to the millpond stretched out before him, keeping an eye on the four people who were wading in the shallows, the ripples lapping at their knees.

I swam. I sat. I wrote. I read. I went for a walk on the pier. I went for another swim. And at the end of all that I still had eight hours in this town before my bus for Airlie Beach left in the evening.

So I decided to get my hair cut. I thought this would be a bit of a quest, but within 5 minutes I found two barbers around the corner from each other. And there was a hairdresser between them. Hervey Bay has a population of just over 50,000. Unless the weather here is incredibly conducive to abnormal hair growth, I couldn't see how it was viable having this many cutters in a shopping precinct that stretched one block. And if there were three serving this tiny part of town, how many were there in the entire place? Was there one haircutter to every five people? Should they have had a sign as you entered town that read: WELCOME TO HERVEY BAY—WOULD YOU LIKE A TRIM?

One establishment was called Terry's and the other was called Danny's. I tossed a coin.

'I was about to have lunch,' Danny told me when I walked in. 'But come in.'

He had a head of thick grey hair cut into a flat-top, and a very neatly manicured beard. When I commented that it was amazing there were two barbers and a hairdresser within spitting distance of each other, Danny looked genuinely puzzled.

'Well, Hervey Bay's a big place, you know.'

I begged to differ, but decided not to bring this up with Danny. After all, he had many sharp objects at hand, and he knew how to use them.

My phone beeped twice while I was in the chair. The first message was from Jeff, and the second was from Sabrina and Martina.

'Hey crazy Barry!' read the Swiss girls' message. 'This place is very "interesting" isn't it?'

They had a nice grasp of sarcasm considering English wasn't their first language.

'We play chess in the park near the "beach". Come say hi if u r round.'

I called Jeff back, and it turned out he was at a nearby café. When I arrived, he was sitting reading a book. It was *The Game,* which he bought earlier that morning, and he was already two chapters in. He was very excited about what it had to say.

'This stuff is gold,' he told me. 'I wish I'd known about it ages ago.'

We found the girls and spent the rest of the afternoon being whipped by them at chess, while joking around and listening to their iPods, which featured a bewildering selection of artists considering they were 19 years old—The Beatles, Portishead, James Blunt, Rod Stewart.

We were all heading to Airlie Beach at different times. The girls were getting the afternoon bus; Jeff was taking the train; I was taking the overnight bus.

We agreed to meet up when we were all up there. After all, we'd known each other for three days. In backpacker time, that's an eternity.

PART 4

AIRLIE BEACH/ THE WHITSUNDAYS

The overnight bus trip from Hervey Bay to Airlie Beach took almost 13 hours and involved the usual run of unnecessary stops every few hours. I slept fitfully, with the sound of rain beating against the window where I was resting my head. It felt like we were on a boat.

We made a stop at 5:30 in the morning at a roadhouse in a place called Ilbilbie. Apart from appearing to have too many i's and l's in its name, the forecourt of the place was littered with rhinoceros beetles that were black, shiny and as big as squash balls. Two Korean girls were so freaked out by them that they wouldn't even walk past to go to the bathroom, instead making a very wide circuit out to the perimeter fence and back. A Swedish girl, perhaps delirious from the bus trip, played with one of the beetles, stroking its back with a finger and talking to it in a girly voice as if she'd just found a puppy.

I just looked at them dumbly, lost in a fog of what I'd come to recognise as 'Greyhound haze'. And then I jumped as someone grabbed my shoulder.

'How's it goin', man?'

It was Tom. He'd been travelling in the bus behind ours.

'This is bizarre, innit?' he said, pointing to the beetles.

'I guess if we were were back at your place in Bondi, they'd all be trapped underneath glasses,' I said.

He laughed, and it sounded like the engine of a Kombi van failing to turn over.

The bus hit the road again and rattled through the rain for another couple of hours, then a mere half hour from our destination we came to a stop. Ahead of us was a long line of vehicles that was not going anywhere. A police car slowly made its way along the line, and the cop informed each driver that as a result of all the rain, the river had risen and cut off the road. He said we'd just have to sit and wait it out until the level dropped.

Our cheery driver, who acted as if this not an inconvenience but a regular feature of the journey, put on a video. It was called *Eight Below,* a family film based on a true story about huskies that survived for months after being abandoned in Antarctica over a particularly harsh winter. It was very Disney, and very sentimental, but perhaps my emotional state by this time was fragile because I kind of choked up a bit while watching it. I was almost disappointed when we started moving again and got to Airlie Beach before the movie finished. I really, really wanted to see the tearful and inevitable reunion between a bunch of shivering canines and the handler who was forced against his better judgement to leave them behind.

The coach conveniently glided through town, past all the hostels and hotels, and kept going. For some reason, the bus station was located in what looked like a vacant lot, on a headland that jutted out into the bay. We disembarked, retrieved our backpacks from the bowels of the bus's storage bay, and then a line of dispirited travellers trudged its way through early morning splotchy rain, back the way we'd just come.

I booked into Magnum's, a hostel that everyone I'd spoken to along the way had mentioned as the largest, loudest, most happening place in town. It's huge, with hut-like dorms in a landscaped jungle setting, and an attached restaurant, beer garden and nightclub. You don't need to leave here for anything, and that's obviously the way they've designed it. After booking in, I found my little hut in my little part of the jungle, dumped my pack and went out to see the town.

Airlie Beach is basically one main strip dotted with hostels, bars, tourist offices and stores aimed at travellers. Because it's so contained, over the next half hour I ran into a bunch of people I'd met earlier in my travels—two Norwegian girls from the Fraser Island trip; an American girl who sat across the aisle from me on the bus from Sydney to Byron Bay; and sure enough, while I was buying sunblock and water in a supermarket...

'How ya doin' man? This place is all right, innit?'

Tom was making up for the time he'd lost to E's, sniff, alcohol and trapping insects under drinking glasses. He'd just booked a big adventure package that would find him hang-gliding, white-water rafting and jumping out of a plane over the next 48 hours.

'What're you up to then?' he asked.

I was heading to Airlie Beach's famous lagoon. So he tagged along.

The lagoon is nicknamed the shagoon or the gene pool because of the various carnal activities backpackers tend to indulge in after-hours. And it's not actually a lagoon. It's a man-made series of pebble-creted pools that have gritty sand and palm trees at the edges. Backpackers are drawn here like thirsty animals to a Kenyan watering hole. There's not a swimming beach here, and although Airlie is the gateway to the 74 islands known as the Whitsundays, the beautiful waters off this part of Queensland are renowned for marine stingers. In January, the temperature hangs around the thirties and the air is wet with humidity, so the lagoon does a roaring trade.

Tom and I found a spot under a palm tree and then he said he had to go and buy a diary.

'Seein' you scribblin' away all the time makes me think I should be gettin' some of this down, know what I mean?' he said.

He asked me to look after his bag and disappeared.

But Airlie Beach being Airlie Beach, I knew it wouldn't be long before someone else I knew would walk—or swim— past. And sure enough, after 10 minutes the Swiss girls floated by.

'Hello! I think we know you!' Martina called out as she breaststroked towards me.

'I told you to stop following me!' I called back.

Martina and Sabrina joined me on my little patch of sand. They were staying at Magnum's too. They'd arrived earlier in the morning, and deciding that there wasn't much to keep them in town for too long, had already booked a couple of days cruising the Whitsundays on a modern maxi yacht, which was leaving the next morning.

The big, sleek maxis had names like *Hammer*, *Condor* and *Freight Train*. There was something called a power catamaran that went under the moniker of *Power Play*. They all sounded like they were named after wrestlers, or the kind of things middle-aged advertising executives put on the personalised number plates of their sports cars. What were these boats trying to prove? Did they—metaphorically speaking—have really small dicks?

I'd decided to go for a 17.5 metre ketch called SV *Whitehaven*. I saw a photo of it with its two masts, its bowsprit (that's the pointy thing out the front, landlubbers) and its old white woodwork contrasted against a setting sun, and felt that this was my kind of speed. It looked like it wasn't trying to impress anyone, but was comfortable with its classic styling (and, once again metaphorically speaking, the size of its dick). And no wanker ever put SV *Whitehaven* on the numberplate of his BMW.

We went for a long swim, sat in the sun for a while, and played some chess.

'Where is Tom?' asked Sabrina. 'He's been gone a long time.'

Indeed, he'd been gone for an hour-and-a-half, and there wasn't enough to do in Airlie Beach to disappear for a quarter of that time.

'Hi Switzerland!' he said when he finally returned and saw the girls. He never seemed to remember anyone's name, instead referred to them by their country of origin.

Did he find a diary?

'Diary?' he asked, looking at me as if he didn't know what I was talking about. 'Oh, no. But me sister rang so I talked to 'er for 'alf an hour. Then I got 'ungry so I went and had some lunch. I'm goin' in! Come on, Switzerland!'

Then he stripped off his shirt and waded into the water with his fists thrust into the air, whistling the theme from *Rocky*.

'I think Tom is a very strange man,' said Sabrina.

It was a packed weekly schedule at the nightclub attached to Magnum's. And it was all high-minded stuff, too.

Mondays and Thursdays were foam party nights, where they filled the dance floor with suds and everyone got slippery. WEAR YA TOGS OR NOTHING AT ALL! screamed the sign.

Tuesdays and Fridays were reserved for wet T-shirt competitions. The sign for that one read: PREPAIR TO GET WET!

Prepair—get it? Whoever was writing this stuff was a genius.

Wednesdays and Saturdays were devoted to jelly wrestling.

And Sunday was toad racing, followed by a singer named Kieran McCarthy. Whoever Kieran McCarthy was, I'm sure he was just thrilled to get second billing to a room full of people betting on which amphibian was going to cross a line first. I wondered if, for a neat segue, Kieran eased into his set by doing Van Halen's 'Jump', or a rendition of Kermit's 'The Rainbow Connection'. Or perhaps for a bit of local flavour, something from Silverchair's debut album, *Frogstomp*.

I'd hit town just in time for a jelly wrestling night. Oh joy. Martina, Sabrina, Tom and my old swimming buddy Jeff, who had texted to say he'd arrived in town, all agreed to meet up to witness the spectacle.

'*The Game* is great!' Jeff told me when we met for an early evening beer. 'I couldn't put it down when I was on the train and I'm already three-quarters of the way through it. And get this. I introduced myself to this Australian girl in the beer garden before, and got a couple of real IOI's from her, then I set up a false time constraint, and I even number closed.'

I couldn't believe it. Jeff had only bought this book yesterday and he was talking like a pick-up artist already. IOI's are indicators of interest, where a girl touches your arm while talking to you or asks your name. A false time constraint lets a woman know that you have places to go and have people to meet, so you say something like 'I have to go and meet a friend now, but maybe we should meet up later'. Number close means that he asked for and got her phone number.

'I'm actually meant to be meeting her for a drink in an hour,' he said.

Was this the same guy whose previous arsenal of pick-up lines extended to 'Fancy a shag?'?

There was a guy playing guitar in the beer garden and after he sang Ben Lee's 'Catch My Disease', he said 'But I hope you don't catch my disease, folks. Just to be safe, there's a chemist a few doors down the road.'

It was priceless stage banter, and as the Swiss girls and Tom had arrived, and he had just launched into 'Sweet Home Alabama', it was obviously time to adjourn to the club.

The place was dark and less than half full, it had a sunken dance floor in the middle, and that's where they'd fashioned a makeshift tub with plastic sheeting, and where they were, at that moment, dumping garbage bins full of jelly.

Half an hour later, a line of eight girls looked sheepishly at the colourless gunk in which they'd soon be rolling.

Our host was wearing a T-shirt that had the word FUNSTER emblazoned across it, so you could immediately tell that he would be no fun whatsoever. He also wore one of those headset microphones, leading me to believe that his T-shirt that read WANKER must have been in the wash.

He worked a rich seam of warm-up material, starting off with some hilarious national stereotyping.

'Do we have any Irish out there tonight?' he yelled.

A round of cheers went up.

'Professional alcoholics!' he shouted with glee.

'Any Canadians in here tonight?'

There were some more scattered cheers, a little less rousing than those beforehand.

'Snap-frozen Yanks!' he exclaimed, to virtually no laughter.

The guy managed to insult all nationalities equally. He would certainly liven up the United Nations if he got a gig there.

'Anyone from the Vatican out there?' I imagined him asking.

Silence.

'Just as well nobody put their hand up, because the Vatican's not a member of the UN! We'd have to get the bouncers to kick your arse all the way back to the Pontiff! He's Catholic, I hear.'

Anyway, back to 'reality' at the nightclub, the Funster was just getting started.

'Tuesday night was a big night at the wet T-shirt competition, folks! Lots of boobies! Which is good, right?'

A couple of cautious cheers. The Funster wasn't happy with this tepid response.

'RIGHT?' he repeated, much louder this time.

A few more cautious cheers.

'But tonight's just as good, 'cos it's about the ladies getting in the jelly pit and beating the shit out of each other, and then hopefully going home and having lesbian sex!'

The cheering got a little more lively.

'Let's start with my favourite part of the game! It's called the lubrication, where the ladies rub jelly all over each other.'

The first two contestants entered the pit. One of them immediately slipped over. Then the two of them half-heartedly stared rubbing jelly on each other.

'Come on, ladies!' yelled the Funster. 'Get into it! And slower! Slower! Yeah, that's right!

'Now the ref is indicating to the crowd that they should ask for a topless fight. What do you reckon? DO WE GET TO SEE BOOBIES?'

No, we didn't. What we saw was a series of women who took their jelly wrestling very seriously indeed. They had sweatbands around their ankles and wrists, and the aim was to remove as many as possible from your opponent. The fighting was determined and fierce, and after a series of knock-out rounds the final was between an attractive, steely-eyed South African called Serena and a compact, smiley Australian named Sam.

The jelly flew from the pit when these two went at it in a blur of gritted teeth and slick, flailing limbs, but after 10 minutes Sam emerged triumphant. She won $250. I found out later that it was her fifth win since arriving in Airlie Beach, and she was helping fund her holiday this way. Perhaps a loss of dignity is worth something after all.

The contest came to an end and the Funster told us to stick around because the music would be pumping until the early hours. The DJ lined up the first song. Of course, it was 'I Don't Feel Like Dancing'.

An hour later I felt a tap on my shoulder. It was Jeff. He was unsuccessfully trying to stifle a big smile.

'And what are you so happy about?' I asked, even though I already knew the answer to my question by the look on his face.

Airlie Beach is the kind of place where little things are big news. Like traffic lights. The place did without them up until recently, when it was announced that two were being installed. The outcry was loud and immediate.

'There was a big protest movement,' said Clare, a middle-aged woman I had met the following morning, who worked in one of the many tourist offices on the main street. 'It mightn't seem like a big thing if you come from Sydney or Melbourne, but here it's just another part of losing our village atmosphere. There's been a lot of development in Airlie Beach, and I don't think it's all been for the good.'

The latest proposal is for a large resort to be built where local shops and a carpark now stand, in a prime piece of land right behind the lagoon. In a place where a couple of traffic lights cause a stir, this was getting some attention.

'It's become a lot less exotic coming to Airlie Beach than it used to be,' said Clare, who has lived here for 14 years. 'It used to be a real destination for travellers, but we're seeing less backpackers than we used to, and they don't stay for as long. There are a lot more places to go in Queensland now as tourism has expanded.

'People come here for a day or two, do their Whitsundays trip, and then leave. And then there's the cruise ship people who just drop in for a day. Airlie Beach is a very transient town.'

Further down the beach I came across the town's tattoo parlour.

'People say Airlie goes off, but it used to be a real party town,' said Tim, the 42-year-old owner, who wore a blue singlet and had an impressive array of ink on his body, including a scorpion that curled its tail around his right eye. 'It's become more upmarket in the 13 years I've been here. The old Airlie was more fun. New Year's Eve especially used to be the bomb, but they had a riot in the 1990s and the police came down on the place after that. And there used to be vacant blocks around here, but not anymore. It's become a lot more developed.'

Tim's two kids were eating some takeaway while he spoke to me, and he noticed that his boy had left a wrapper on the ground outside the shop.

'Jasper, can you please pick up that rubbish and put it in the bin?' he asked gently. 'Good boy.'

Tim said that 60 to 70 per cent of his clients were female, and that the most common tattoos backpackers wanted were Chinese and Egyptian symbols, and stars, particularly the Southern Cross.

'It's like a souvenir,' he said. 'They can go back home and say "I got that in Airlie Beach" or "I got this in Byron".'

I wandered back to Magnum's and noticed a bunch of people in the beer garden simulating sex with each other. Does it say something about how far I'd come on this journey that I was not taken aback by this sight?

Then I heard a voice call out 'Kangaroo!' and they changed position. I turned the corner and there was the guy in the FUNSTER T-shirt, headset microphone firmly in place. He was playing a game with the backpackers where they had to assume different sex positions in the style of various Australian animals, in order to win free drinks.

It was definitely time to get on a boat and not come back for a while.

Whenever I step onto a boat with the knowledge that I will have to spend at least the next three hours on it, quite naturally my mind turns to *Gilligan's Island*. *(For some reason I have decided to mention Gilligan's Island three times during this story. Apart from being a most excellent sitcom from the 1960s, I can't think why I have this obsession with it, apart from the fact that along with Marcia Brady and Catwoman, Ginger Grant played a large part in my sexual awakening as a boy. Anyway, one reference down, two to go.)*

As the jaunty and informative theme song pointed out, the hapless passengers on the SS *Minnow* were meant to be on a three-hour tour. To ram home the point, and probably to add some sense of foreboding, the song actually repeated that phrase 'a three-hour tour'. Because, as we all know, the weather started getting rough, the tiny ship was tossed, and to cut a long story short, these people ended up being castaways on an island from 1964 to 1967.

Subsequently, organised events involving large numbers of people thrown together on aquatic vessels were never my idea of a good time. As a rule I like to arrive at social gatherings late and leave when I damn well want to without all those awkward, drawn-out goodbyes. On a boat cruise you can't arrive late, and depending on your swimming skills and the prevalence of sharks, you can't leave whenever you damn well want to. One year, a magazine I work for held their Christmas party on a boat cruise, thus combining my two worst nightmares in one. In fact, hell for me will turn out to be an eternal work Christmas party held on a boat. With Celine Dion playing live.

I wasn't going to hell quite yet. I was going to the Whitsundays, and for the next three days, my life would in the hands of a man with wild eyes, messed-up hair and a snaggle-tooth smile.

As recommended by the tour company, I packed a few bits of clothing and toiletries into one green supermarket recyclable bag, cans of beer into another, and took the long walk that hugged the bay around Airlie Beach and ended up at the marina. And there was my home for the next two nights and three days—the SV *Whitehaven*. A deckhand named Josh, a cook named Angela and Richard, our illustrious captain, greeted us at the dock. Angela started calling the roll. There were 15 of us—over half were British, there were a couple of Canadians, a couple of Zimbabweans, an American and me.

'Erica?' called out Angela.

No one responded.

'Erica?' she repeated.

Nothing again.

'Does anyone know an Erica?' she asked.

No one did.

Five minutes later, as we were about to board, Erica turned up. She had been sitting through a preamble from another crew at another wharf and was just about to board another boat when they checked off names and realised she was in the wrong place. She had big brown eyes, a cute upturned nose, long legs and shiny brown hair. Naturally I assumed I wouldn't speak to her for the entire trip.

Instead, after we boarded and sleeping quarters were assigned, it turned out we were in the same cabin of five, squeezed into the bow of the boat on narrow tiered bunks that curved to the shape of the hull. Within 10 minutes we found ourselves sitting next to each other filling out forms about our medical history. We were going to be snorkelling over the next three days so the crew needed to know if there were any reasons any of us may end up as sinkers rather than floaters. She was writing a lot down and gave me a bit of a worried look.

'I'm not sure how much of this I should tell them because they mightn't let me in the water,' she said.

And then she told me her story. She was 26 years old and came from Seattle. Five years ago she was on her way home with some friends in a car. She was asleep in the back. They passed through an intersection and another car came straight through a stop sign and barrelled into them. Erica spent the next three days in a coma, and the next month in hospital. She still had to take medication every day as she was at risk from seizures.

'If I vague out over the next few days, you'll know that it's just my brain,' she told me. 'I sometimes forget things. Sorry, I've forgotten your name already.'

I told her not to worry as this was a common affliction among women, whether they'd suffered brain trauma or not.

We went back on deck in time to see the boat motor past the breakwater off Airlie Beach, and I got to know the crew.

Josh was from Saltspring Island in Canada and had been working as a deckhand for three months. He knew about tying knots from his experience as a climber, but had never worked on a boat before, and had learned on the job.

Angela had been a cook on the SV *Whitehaven* for four months.

'But I'm ready to move on from Airlie Beach now,' she admitted.

'Is four months about the limit for the place?' I asked.

'Less than that, really,' she said. 'It's a very small town. And I'm from Tasmania! Back at Airlie there's not much to do apart from going out and getting drunk, or playing barefoot bowling. And I haven't been barefoot bowling.'

Perhaps there do exist captains of boats who are not slightly eccentric, but Richard wasn't adding to their number. He was droll and genial, and fond of a one-liner and a tall story. Within the first hour he spouted the following:

- Has anyone ever seen a dugong? They look like a bulldog that has eaten a wasp.
- Green turtles start sexual activity about the age of 40, much like Australian men.
- Those jellyfish you can see down there are 95 per cent water and pretty dim. They're very much like surfers from the Gold Coast in that respect.

Having never been a figure skater, a competitive swimmer or a participant in Sydney's Mardi Gras parade, I have managed to get through life thus far without wearing lycra. That was about to change.

A couple of hours after leaving port, the boat anchored at Blue Pearl Bay, a sheltered alcove on the north-western side of Hayman Island. Before entering the water, we were told to swathe ourselves in tight-fitting body suits and hoods. The reason for this is the presence of something you can barely see unless you look very closely in the water. Box jellyfish and Irukandji are transparent, and the latter can be as small as 1 centimetre in length, so they're virtually impossible to spot until they're almost right on top of you. And if you're not wearing a lycra stinger suit, you definitely do not want one on top of you. Depending on the species they can cause heart attack, central nervous system seizures, and—one of my least favourite afflictions—death. In fact, a box jellyfish only has to get a few of its 60 tentacles wrapped around half your arm and you could be belly-up in minutes.

As you may be able to tell, I researched this topic quite a bit as I'm not a fan of immersing myself into a body of water where heart attacks and central nervous system seizures are possible side effects. The official stinger season runs from October to May (I was there bang in the middle, in January) but the experts say that there's a year-round risk.

All of which begs the question: why on earth would anyone want to swim here at all? Well, there are a number of reasons. It's beautiful, idyllic, the water is clear and clean, and it's teeming with marine life that is very nice to look at that—unlike the aforementioned jellyfish—doesn't kill you.

But the reality is that few people are stung by jellyfish and even fewer die. In fact, the Whitsunday Marine Stinger Management Committee, which was set up in 2006, picked apart many of the fears surrounding the stingers. Dr Lisa-ann Gershwin, a national advisor on the subject, reported that there were just three known deaths from Irukandji in the last century, the same number as the national death toll from swans in the same period. And no one sees parents dressing up their kids in swan-protective suits when they go to the local pond with a bag full of stale bread.

Still, I did find it strange that the thing to do if you happen to get stung is to apply vinegar to the area. As a remedy to the diagnosis 'death within minutes', the term 'apply some vinegar' seems a bit like throwing a box of band-aids to someone who has just had their arm ripped off by a shark.

With these pleasant visions and statistics dancing in my head, I slipped on my flippers, donned my face mask and snorkel, and jumped over the side of the boat. And within 10 minutes I saw Elvis. I even touched him. He felt like a big wet pineapple.

Elvis is a Maori wrasse, a fish that is over a metre long, weighs more than 40 kilograms, has big blue-green scales and a bump on his forehead. He's so large and placid, with unblinking eyes the size of large buttons, that he seems almost prehistoric. And the fact that I could just float there looking like Aquaman's geeky sidekick, and get close enough to reach out and touch him, just made the whole thing seem more surreal.

In fact, as you float through the water in this part of the world, idly kicking your flippered feet and breathing through a snorkel, everything does seem other-worldly. Even the soundtrack is strange. All you can hear is your own breathing and the scratchy clatter of the fish nibbling at the coral. These corals can be metres across and they have curvy, undulating, amorphous shapes that are reflected in their names—brain, stag, plate, bubble and mushroom. Their vibrant colours—reds, blues, oranges, pinks—all seem like they're not of the earth. After a few minutes gliding through this environment it seems like you're floating weightlessly through space and surveying the surface of another planet.

And then there are the harlequin tuskfish, parrot fish, long-nosed butterfly fish—even their names give you some idea of the Dr Seuss-like nature of their design. Occasionally a school of hundreds of demoiselles and damsels swim past, an ephemeral flutter of small silver and blue fish flashing all around your body. You can reach out and get a fingertip or two to their little fins and bodies before they skitter away.

We all returned to the boat tired and happy an hour later, our skin salty and wrinkled from the water, swapping tales of what we saw as if we'd suddenly joined the Cousteau family. Josh pulled up anchor and Richard turned the boat towards Hook Island. We drank tea, snacked on biscuits and fruit, and got to know each other.

Every backpacker conversation you ever have follows pretty much the same path, signposted by the following questions:

1) How long have you been here in (insert name of town/city)?
2) Where are you from?
3) Where have you been before now?
4) Where are you headed after this?
5) How long have you been in Australia?
6) How long are you staying in Australia?
7) Want a drink?

After the first few days of travelling, you start to get a bit self-conscious about the fact that this sequence occurs pretty much every time you meet somebody new. After a couple of weeks you just accept that this is how it happens and roll with it. Just as the east coast run is a path that everyone seems to follow, the backpacker-to-backpacker start-up conversation (which I shall henceforth refer to, and possibly trademark as B2B S-U Con) is a blueprint that everyone adheres to.

Sometimes it can veer off before getting through all the steps. For instance, if it's three o'clock in the morning in the middle of a bar and the two participants in the B2B S-U Con are inebriated enough, it could go like this:

1) How long have you been here in (insert name of town/city)?
2) It's hot in here, isn't it?
3) Indecipherable carnal noises coming from the bushes/lagoon/upper bunk 10 minutes later.

Or in the case of one particularly memorable conversation I had with a 21-year-old girl from Canberra, who was reading a book by new-age storyteller Paulo Coelho:

1) How long have you been here in Hervey Bay?
2) Where are you from?
3) Do you believe in God?

Suffice to say, as she was the one who asked that last question, she did believe in God. She also believed that the earth was created in literally seven days. It's usually polite to get to at least point six in the B2B S-U Con before expressing deeply held religious views.

That first afternoon on the boat I got to know three girls who came from Hertfordshire, outside of London. They spoke in horsey accents, and like many groups of girls I met travelling together, they fell into almost sitcom-like character types. Emma was the cute little blonde one. Mel was the tomboyish smart-alec one. Vashti was the bubbly, flirtatious one.

'English girls have a reputation for drinking a lot and being easy,' said Vashti. 'And I must say, it's well deserved.'

I liked these girls from that point on.

The three of them referred to the *Lonely Planet* guide to Australia as *The Planet,* and they took turns looking after their shared copy so they knew where it was at all times.

'We live by *The Planet,*' said Vashti. 'It's our Bible.'

'The one day we didn't use it, we ended up at this terrible restaurant run by a horrible woman called Denise,' added Mel. 'She had a really bad blonde dye job, and the food was absolutely disgusting.

'So that was the last time,' says Emma. 'Now we only go by *The Planet.*'

But by following *The Planet* so strictly, did they think they were experiencing much of the real Australia at all, or were they just on some sort of moveable, insulated ride surrounded by other travellers?

'You don't necessarily come here to experience the normal Australia,' said Vashti. 'It's backpacker Australia. You bond with other travellers because you're all doing the same things. Skydiving, for instance. You can do that pretty much anywhere, but you do it here because everyone else is.'

Would you even think about skydiving at home in England?

'It's something you talk about and something that you'd always like to do, but you don't necessarily end up doing it,' said Mel. 'But when you're travelling you have the time frame and other people around you who are doing it. Plus at home you'd be doing it in Oxford, so you'd be coming down going, 'Oooh look! There's a field! And another field! And another field! And a canal! And another field!"

It was already almost dark by the time we got to Nara Inlet, a bay of Hook Island, where we anchored for the night, then had dinner and broke open our alcohol supplies.

There's something romantic about being itinerant, and being on a boat only ups the ante. Gravity feels lighter, responsibilities lift, inhibitions fade. We see sunsets all the time but they seem that much more intense and filled with meaning when we're away, surrounded by people who up until very recently were complete strangers.

And travellers build up intimacy with each other very quickly. As John, the Englishman back in Bondi had said, you can know someone for two days and trust them with your passport and your wallet.

But you also entrust people with things that are much more private—secrets and dreams and hopes and fears.

On Fraser Island, I'd struck up an easy friendship with an English girl named Julie. She was in her early thirties, and she came from Swindon. The first day we met, our group was traipsing through the rainforest on a walk, surrounded by the buzz of insects. After stopping to photograph a goanna, we got talking and out of nowhere she started telling me all about her recent divorce, and how everyone felt it was her fault.

Five days later, when I first walked into my room at the hostel in Airlie Beach, I'd met an 18-year-old Canadian girl who was lying on the bunk below mine, reading *Catch Me If You Can*. Within 10 minutes, she was sobbing and telling me about her father, who had just been diagnosed with cancer. She'd been planning to travel for six months, but now she'd decided to do a whirlwind four weeks and then get home to be with him, even though he was trying to convince her to stick to her original plan.

And later that first night on the boat in the Whitsundays I was dangling my feet over the side with Vashti. While we watched fish churn up the inky black water below us, leaving trails of phosphorescence in their wake, she revealed that she'd been going out with a guy for seven months. She'd started up with him only five days after breaking up with her ex. She had Indian heritage and her ex ticked all the right boxes—right caste, her parents liked him, they'd already been together a few years. But there was no chemistry. The new guy was white. She still hadn't told her ex that she was seeing someone new, and didn't know what to do about this.

I wondered aloud how she couldn't tell him, yet she could tell an Australian she'd only known less than a day.

'It's easier to tell someone you don't know about all that stuff, especially when you're travelling,' she said. 'Besides, I'll probably never see you again after we get off this boat.'

She was wrong there, but that's another story.

Just then, Richard announced to everyone he was turning in for the night.

'But remember,' he said. 'Tomorrow morning we're setting off at four...no five...yeah, five minutes past seven.'

The moonlight glinted off his crooked smile as he disappeared below deck. The combination of the sun, the snorkelling, the salt air, and the constant movement of the boat through the water all day, meant that we weren't far behind him, and by ten o'clock, everyone was tucked into their little bunks. It was the earliest I'd been in bed since starting this trip.

The next day we experienced what many guide books and travel experts tell us is possibly the planet's most beautiful beach, and what no guide books or travel experts tell us are the planet's most annoying flies.

After breakfast we pulled up anchor and cruised to Tongue Bay, an inlet of Whitsunday Island. The rubber dinghy with outboard motor attached ferried us to shore, and then we entered the world of a William Golding novel.

The flies were fat, brown, and around 2 centimetres long. And when they bit you, which appeared to be the main reason for their existence, it felt like the head of a recently extinguished match was being pressed into your flesh.

You'd slap at them, and if you got a direct hit, they'd look a little stunned, shake themselves off, then stare you down with an expression that said 'is that all you've got, human?' These were tough flies. And on the bushwalk from Tongue Bay, climbing up over the headland, they were everywhere.

The hot, sweaty trek—punctuated with the percussive sound of 18 people slapping themselves and calling out in surprise and pain when bitten—was worth it when we got to the summit of the headland, to a place called Eagles Nest. Below us was a stretch of blinding white sand fringing blue water. Directly in front was Hill Inlet, and around to the left was our boat's namesake—Whitehaven Beach. To call it postcard perfect is cliché, but postcards of this exact view are often used to advertise the charms of Queensland.

As we took it all in, Josh told us that the sand here was almost 100 per cent pure silica. It's so fine that you can use it to polish silver, it could be used to make glass, and it will completely ruin the insides of your camera if you let those fine granules anywhere near it. It was almost too blinding to look at in the midday sun, and when you walked on it, your feet made squeaking noises, like the squelching sound of Astroboy's robot-boy legs in the old TV cartoons.

Once we got down on the beach we entered the warm, clear water, although the full effect was dulled a little by the fact we had to wear stinger suits. Schools of small silver fish darted backwards and forwards, and we spotted a couple of stingrays lazing in the shallows, prompting everyone to make terrible Steve Irwin jokes. Apparently tragedy plus time does equal comedy.

Sample:

You'd think Steve Irwin would have worn sunscreen, wouldn't you?

To protect him from the harmful rays.

Okay, perhaps tragedy plus time equals really lame comedy.

The water was so flat, shallow, warm and clear that after about half an hour there wasn't really much else to do but get out again. Being Australian, I sat in the shade of a tree. As the others were not Australian, they spent the next hour-and-a-half in direct sunlight, lying on their backs and then their fronts to make sure the melanomas were evenly spread.

Later on our return, while waiting on the beach to be picked up by the dinghy, a few of us had a competition to see how many flies we could kill by just standing there and whacking them when they landed on our bodies. One of the Zimbabweans won with 48 kills—we'd been waiting for the boat for only around 15 minutes.

The remainder of the day passed in a pleasant, lazy routine of cruising, eating, chatting, snorkelling at Mantaray Bay on the northern side of Hook Island, and just doing that thing where you look out across the blue expanse dotted with green islands, thinking vague and hazy thoughts about what a beautiful place this planet can be when we let it.

That night we moored at Stonehaven, another sheltered bay on Hook Island, and after dinner, Richard invited us out to the front of the boat. He wanted to talk about the stars.

Once we were assembled, he produced a laser pointer from his pocket and started picking constellations out of the sky and talking about them. This immediately elicited oohs and aahs, because even though the laser was something you could probably pick up in a two-dollar store on a keyring, out here in a patch of water off Queensland at nine o'clock at night, it pierced the darkness and actually served its purpose of pointing out celestial pinpricks of light scattered all over the velvety black sky.

I'd always found the whole astronomy thing a bit of mumbo jumbo. Our science teachers back in high school used to point out that these three stars obviously make up the belt of the god Orion, and that handful of stars obviously look like a crab. And I'd stare and squint and stare again, but they still looked like totally random sprinklings of twinkly things to me.

But Richard was entertaining and informative, and had the good humour to admit that 'they were off their heads on magic mushrooms when they named some of these things', which was something my science teachers back in high school definitely never said.

There was a nice moment when he tried to describe the vastness of space. I was sitting with a rotund English guy called John to my left and the aforementioned American girl Erica to my right.

'Let's pretend you're a galaxy, John,' said Richard. 'And you're another galaxy, Baz.'

Yes, like Beautiful Al back in Bondi, he was the kind of guy who started calling me Baz within 60 seconds of meeting him.

'And you're another galaxy, Erica. Now, between John and Baz there might be two million light years. That means it takes two million years for light to travel between those two galaxies. Between Baz and Erica there might be three million light years.

'That's just three galaxies, but there are literally millions of these galaxies in the universe. Now, how many light years do you think man has made it into space?'

There were random guesses that were way too high.

'We've gone one light second,' said Richard. 'We've walked on the moon, and it takes one second for light to get from the moon to the earth.'

He waited a beat for everyone to take this in.

'Space is big, people,' he said quietly. 'Space is appropriately named.'

He went on to tell a story about his young son, who lived with his mother, and about the star they decided was his personal star. When his son looked at it every night, he knew that his father was looking at it too, even though they now lived 2000 miles apart. It was dark when he told us this, but you could almost see every woman on the boat swoon.

'I tell you, guys, learn about the stars,' Richard said. 'This is great stuff for picking up girls.'

A bottle of tequila was passed around later in the evening, and one by one, our little group started drifting off to bed. As it was such a warm night, some decided to simply crash on the deck rather than go below. Everyone had noticed that Simon, an Englishman who was six feet seven tall, had made a concerted play for Erica during the afternoon, and the two had been canoodling for much of the day.

I turned in around eleven o'clock, but within half an hour, I was woken by two of the English girls who had been trying to sleep on deck. They were complaining as they bumped around, attempting to find their bunks in the dark. I asked what was wrong.

'Those two are really going for it up there,' said one. 'It's disgusting.'

It turned out the new couple was getting on even better than everyone suspected. It was going to be a bumpy night.

Morning broke on our last day—Australia Day. After breakfast the only three Australians on board—Richard the captain, Angela the cook, and me—were cajoled into singing the anthem while everyone stood at attention. As anthems go, 'Advance Australia Fair' is a shocker. It's not really rousing at all, the tune is pretty lame and the lyrics (especially that bit about our land being 'girt by sea') sound outdated and uninspiring. And I don't know anyone who knows the second verse. We had trouble getting through the first verse in time and in tune.

After breakfast we suited up for one last time, and jumped over the side for a final snorkel, but the water seemed to be churned up by currents and visibility wasn't as clear as it had been the day before. Still, after being on a boat with people for two days, I enjoyed being submerged in the water for half an hour, lazily kicking my flippers, listening to my heartbeat and the blood rushing in my ears.

'A couple of years ago I was taking tourists out on a boat around here and on the horizon I could see a whale surface,' Richard told us, after we'd got back on board and he'd manoeuvred the boat out of the bay and pointed it back towards Airlie Beach. 'I tried to keep an eye on it for a while, but it disappeared, and then the next thing it was right alongside the boat. It just stopped there with its tail up out of the water and it didn't move. I told everyone on the boat that it must be sick because I'd never seen a whale do anything like this.

'Then all of a sudden there were all these bubbles everywhere, followed by all this blood. And finally this little whale that was so small it looked like a dolphin came up to the surface. It was just the most amazing thing. They stayed for a little while, and then the mother breached fully, with her tail clearing the water, which is unusual because that behaviour is usually associated with males. And then the baby whale breached too, as if it was learning from its mother already.

'I'm not one of those people who believe this sort of thing, but I swear it put this aura over the whole boat. It was a pretty special day.'

We didn't see any whales, but a half hour later, we did see some dolphins frolicking to starboard, their wet, sleek bodies sliding in and out of the water.

The closer we got to Airlie Beach, the quieter everyone seemed to get. Photos were taken, email addresses were swapped, arrangements were made to meet up later that night.

Torgeir was the first person I met after I booked back into Magnum's in Airlie Beach, and walked into my new room. It was the early afternoon and he was lying on his bed. There's always someone lying on their bed looking tired in the early afternoon in backpacker hostels, but Torgeir had a pretty good excuse.

He'd been riding his bike. From Cairns. Which is 634 kilometres north of Airlie Beach.

Torgeir—which is pronounced tou-gey-rare—was from Norway, and until recently he was a professional soccer player, playing on the wing for a team called Sogdal. He quit because he wanted to see the world. He started by taking three weeks off to hang around Barbados, then came to Australia. He got it into his head that he wanted to ride a pushbike all the way down the Australian east coast, from Cairns to Melbourne, and he'd set out two weeks before I met him. It's over 3000 kilometres from Cairns to Melbourne, so I guessed that Torgeir had a lot of experience riding a bike.

'No, not really,' he said.

You're joking, right?

'No,' he said. As I mentioned, he was from Norway, so he didn't joke around much. 'I rode a bike when I was a kid, but I've never had a racing bike and I haven't really trained to do this.'

Then why do it?

He looked at me for a moment. I wondered if no one had ever asked him this question, and if this was the first time he'd had to rack his brain for the reasoning behind his quest.

'I want to test myself,' he finally said. 'I want to see if I can do it. I do get a little bit scared on the highways, and being alone for long periods of time is not always easy. Also, it can get dangerous on the road with the big trucks going past. Three days ago, one truck actually touched the bags on the side of my bike as it went past.'

He cycled up to nine hours a day, riding for two-and-a-half hours at a time without a break. The average daytime temperature in January in that part of Queensland is around 30°C. I felt overheated and exhausted walking down the street in Airlie Beach. And it's not a long street. Torgeir would go through 18 litres of water a day. And if it wasn't the heat he was battling, it was the tropical rain.

'Do you remember when it was raining so hard a few days ago?' he asked.

I did. I was sitting in a warm, dry bus between Hervey Bay and Airlie Beach. Admittedly, it was warm with the body odour, sweat and farts of other travellers crammed into a metal canister on wheels, and we were trapped on it for 13 hours, but I was not riding a bike in the rain that was belting down outside. I was watching a movie about huskies.

'I was trying to ride in that rain, and at times it was so hard that it seemed impossible to me that I would make it to the next town. But you just have to laugh and get through it. There's no doubt you learn about yourself doing something like this.'

Right then the door flew open, and there was a wafting smell of sweat and cigarettes, followed by a hulk of a guy with a duffel bag swinging from his shoulder.

'Which bed is free?'

I put a question mark at the end of that sentence, because I suppose it was a question. But it sounded more like a demand. I pointed to a bed across from mine. He dumped his bag next to it and then flopped down on the bed so it bounced a few times.

'How are you doing?' I asked.

'I haven't slept in three weeks,' he mumbled in an Australian accent.

'Partying?' I ventured.

'I wish,' he replied.

He was from Cairns, and he was the skipper of a crew that had been salvaging a seven million dollar boat that sank off Mackay. They had worked around the clock, grabbing an hour's shut-eye every now and then.

'You guys don't like air-conditioning, do you?' he asked us. Once again it sounded more like a demand than a question. 'I hate it. Recycled air. One person has the flu, everyone in the room gets it. So if we can keep it off, that'd be good. And neither of you snore, do you?'

We barely had time to answer before he fell into a heavy slumber.

After doing some much-needed laundry and having an even more needed long, hot shower (we were limited to 1 minute showers on the boat), I was lying in my bunk having a half hour nap before going out to meet the Whitsundays crew for the evening. All I could hear were some frogs in the garden outside.

And then, quietly at first, I heard stirrings coming from the English guy in the bunk below me. He mumbled something about a ukelele.

I didn't know what to say. Was he striking up a conversation with me? I pretended I couldn't hear him.

But he kept going. He mumbled 'you're my little lady, lady, lady, love me.'

Now I realised that he had his MP3 player on and was singing along to a song. He was a pretty bad singer. But what was that song?

There was some mention of curtains, a rainy day outside, and...banana pancakes! Incredible. There was no escape.

It was Jack Johnson, the ex-surfer who had been taken under Ben Harper's wing, and had then broken out into the mainstream, becoming the soundtrack (along with 'I Don't

Feel Like Dancing', of course) to every single place I ventured into that even had a glimpse of beach through the window. For decades Bob Marley had served this purpose. But good old Jack, with his strummed acoustic guitar, his I'm-not-quite-awake-yet voice, and his sing-songy lyrics about lazy days and warm relationships, had become the aural backdrop to everything from buying bread to sipping a beer in any coastal town between Bondi and Cairns.

In fact, the former Hawaii resident had apparently bought a place in Byron Bay, where 'Banana Pancakes', with its drowsy feel and lyrics about wanting to stay inside and fool around and then eat—yes, you guessed it—banana pancakes, could be the local anthem.

In cafés, on the radio, in bars, in convenience stores—he was always there. Someone would pick up an acoustic guitar and there he was again. Even out on the boat, floating around the Whitsundays, the first thing that came on the sound system when it was cranked up was this guy.

And perhaps there exists a contract that every covers band and beer garden singer-guitarist up and down the east coast of Australia must sign. They have to agree to do at least one Jack Johnson song, one Bob Marley song, and all of the following—Oasis's 'Wonderwall', Lynyrd Skynyrd's 'Sweet Home Alabama', the Violent Femmes' 'Blister In The Sun', Van Morrison's 'Brown Eyed Girl', Green Day's 'Good Riddance (Time Of Your Life)' and the Counting Crows' 'Mr Jones'.

Musicians playing in towns that were hundreds of miles apart would have almost exactly the same setlist, and it would elicit the same enthusiastic response from the well-oiled crowd. Like Pavlov's dogs and the sound of a bell, 'Wonderwall' would always cause English backpackers to salivate.

They were called Shakers and I'm not exactly sure what was in them, but all of a sudden everyone seemed a lot friendlier. Shakers came in plastic cocktail shakers, which we dispensed into shot glasses and then skulled.

I was standing in a crowded Irish bar—because you had to have an Irish bar in a sub-tropical beachside town, of course. A dozen of the die-hards from our Whitsundays trip were getting to know each other better on dry land. In our little group were the English girls (Vashti, Emma and Mel), an Englishman named Ian (whose buddy John had gone a bit too fast a bit too early, and combined with his unenviable overexposure to the sun, had retired early) and Paulo, a Spanish guy from Barcelona, who I'd invited to tag along with our group for the night. Paulo hadn't been on our boat—I'd met him in the beer garden at the hostel. He was sitting there collecting slang Australian words and phrases, including 'root', 'stubbie', 'got the munchies', and 'pulling your leg', and writing them in his notebook. I told him that if he became proficient in these, then he'd sound like a stereotyped character from a bad Australian movie from the early 1970s.

Paulo taught Spanish to foreign kids at home and had told his boss that he wanted to come to Australia to improve his

English. He really wanted to spend all his time surfing and meeting girls. He ended up having sex with his English teacher in Byron Bay and cracking his rib after being dumped in the surf. So we had one thing in common.

'We live only one time,' he told me. 'And I will remember all my life my trip to Australia and sleeping with my teacher and breaking my rib surfing.'

After a few rounds of Shakers, the temperature of the room went up and things started getting nicely fuzzy around the edges. Arms started snaking around waists, lips started brushing cheeks, there was much flashing of teeth and batting of eyelids. So we ordered another round.

We gravitated to the dance floor, where a fairly average covers band was playing 'Blister In The Sun'. Then they did 'Mr Jones'. Then they did 'Brown Eyed Girl'. They were following the script and I felt like I was Bill Murray in *Groundhog Day*.

Vashti and I were getting pretty friendly at this point.

'You do know I have a boyfriend at home that I've been with for seven months, right?' she asked.

I explained that I was aware of this as she'd already mentioned it 134 times since I'd met her 72 hours ago.

Then she hugged me. Then she started flirting with Ian, so I left them to it.

Paulo and I pulled up a couple of seats at the bar and watched the band for a while.

'That English girl you are with,' he said. 'You know how she keeps talking about her boyfriend back at home?'

'Yeah, I had noticed that.'

'We have a saying in Spanish for people like this. *Amor de lejos, amor de pendejos.*'

'What does it mean?' I asked.

'Faraway love is the love of idiots.'

I liked that.

Erica the American came in with Simon, the six foot seven Englishman. People kept staring at him. Complete strangers came up to give him the old 'How's the weather up there?' line, which he took with surprising good humour, considering he could have snapped their puny necks with his tree-trunk arms. One guy shook his hand and congratulated him on being so tall, and another actually bought him a beer. I never realised before that being of freakish height could get you free drinks.

After half an hour the word went out that it was time to cross the road to go to a club called Mama Africa's. Vashti disengaged herself from Ian and grabbed my hand.

'Let's go, Bazmotron!' she said. 'To Mama Africa's!'

Ian gave me a look that asked, 'What the fuck is going on here?' Or possibly threatened, 'I'll see you outside, buddy.'

I shrugged and gave him an insipid smile that I hoped said, 'I'm as much in the dark as you are, buddy.'

At Mama Africa's things became messier. The soundtrack was the insistent and anonymous thump of techno, and everyone had been drinking for hours, and we just walked straight in the door, hit the dance floor and didn't leave.

Eventually the English girls decided to call it a night. Vashti came over and put two hands on my shoulders.

'I wish I was a mind reader, Bazmotron,' she said.

'And why's that?'

'So I could guess what the hell you're thinking.'

'Sometimes I guess you just have to use your imagination,' I replied.

Jesus. Those Shakers were stronger than I thought. It was like we were reciting dialogue from some bad movie.

She kissed me on one cheek then the other, and then the first one again. Then she moved her mouth to my ear.

'I hope we'll be seeing you in Cairns,' she said.

Then she went and said goodbye to Ian. This wasn't a competition. But I noticed that she spent less time saying goodbye to him than she did with me.

A few minutes later it was just Ian and me.

'Are you still going to hang around?' I asked.

'If you are, mate,' he said. 'Not sure what was going on there. I think she was playing both of us. You want a beer?'

I did. We hit the dance floor again and started dancing with two more English girls, one blonde, one brunette. We had one more beer after that, and then left.

Outside the rain had started to come down. We were hot and sweaty and drunk and tired. Ian was staying in a different hostel, so we started to go our separate ways.

'Good luck with your travels, mate,' Ian said. 'I wish you could have got off with her. I wish I could have got off with her more. But if I didn't, then fair play to you.'

The English can certainly be very polite and sporting when they want to be.

Then he scrawled his email address in my notebook and we hugged, two stupid males at two o'clock in the morning, bonded by sweat, exhaustion, alcohol, wanderlust and idiocy.

PART 5

CAIRNS

I woke up the next morning to the sound of Torgeir eating bananas and drinking water. It sounded a lot louder than eating bananas and drinking water should. It sounded like the late John Bonham from Led Zeppelin was playing a drum solo inside my skull, and he was going to be doing it for some time.

I looked across the room and the salvaging guy was still dead to the world. He didn't appear to have shifted a centimetre since he spoke to us the evening before.

Torgeir was getting ready to hit the road on his bike, so we talked for a while on the verandah. I asked him what he thought about when he was out there for so many hours by himself.

'Actually, I speak to myself in English, because I want to practise my language skills while I am here,' he said.

I couldn't help admiring the guy. He said he was happy that someone was interested in what he was doing.

'When I first came here, the day before I met you, I booked into a double room here at Magnum's, and my roommate was from England,' he said. 'He was so different to me. He just drank beer and smoked marijuana all day. I couldn't understand what he was doing here, and I could not even understand what he said a lot of the time. I had to move out of there.'

And now Torgeir had to move out of here. He wanted to make it to Mackay today, and that was 150 kilometres away. I wished him luck and took some photos of him setting off. Then I packed up my stuff, booked out of the hostel, and trekked through town to get to the bus station. The rain had cleared and it was already hot in the early hours of the day. I was sweating and had the beginnings of a headache by the time I got there, ready to ride the dog one last time.

Bus drivers on Greyhounds must go through a demanding training process in order to learn how to speak so tortuously into a microphone. They must repeat the same instruction over and over in slightly different ways. And they must...leave long...and inconsistent...gaps...between the...words that...they slowly string...together.

'We'll be disembarking the bus...in Townsville...soon,' droned Len, our driver from Airlie Beach. 'It's now...22 minutes to two. We'll be stopping .. .and getting back on the bus...at 2:15. That's...a quarter past two. And then...we'll be leaving...at...2:25. That's twenty-five past two. Remember not to bring...any hamburgers...pies...or other...hot food onto the coach. No unopened drinks...milk...or milk products…and remember…the bus is leaving at twenty-five past two…that's 2:25.'

I worried that Len had perhaps been on the road a little too long without a break. He made interminable, disconnected announcements that didn't seem to be of any importance whatsoever. And he'd leave such long gaps between sentences that you'd think he was finished, and then be jolted back awake as he continued on his meandering way.

The Canadian girl next to me was in tears from laughing so much. All I had to say were the words 'milk' and 'milk products' and she was reduced to a quivering mess.

At Townsville, Len left us and we got a new driver—Kev the comedian.

'There's a toilet down the back,' he told us in the first 10 minutes of his introductory lecture. 'Remember that just like the coach, it stops at traffic lights and goes around corners. If you do fall off while you're sitting on the toilet, let out a scream and someone will come and knock the door down, we'll take pictures and video you, and play it at the next Christmas party. You should have seen last year's. It was an absolute cracker.

'Oh, and no drinking alcohol or taking drugs on the coach. I get way too envious. And by the way, if you need any questions answered or need advice on your love life or finances, come down and ask me. We'll see what we can do.'

We left Airlie Beach at nine in the morning. Every two-and-a-half hours we stopped for a 30- or 40-minute break at a roadhouse or bus terminal. At Cardwell, a small town where we stopped two hours north of Townsville, it was mango country. You could tell this because the toilets were not marked Ladies and Gents, but Mangoes and No Mangoes. Some of the backpackers looked confused as they stood outside, wondering which place to enter.

It was half past eight at night by the time we rolled into Cairns, which straight-away looked bigger and brasher than Airlie Beach or Hervey Bay. The streets were wider, there were more of them, the buildings were taller and more densely packed, and neon signs hanging in front of stores advertised everything from didgeridoos to Ken Done designed clothing.

'Don't do anything I wouldn't do,' Kev said as he handed out backpacks from the bus's cargo bay, and I wandered off looking for a place called Gilligan's.

There's an easy way to tell if you're staying in an upmarket hostel. Is your key made of metal and attached to a cheap plastic tag? Or is it a swipe card on a coloured cloth lanyard that you can hang around your neck? If it's the latter, then you know you're not staying in a backpacker hostel, you're staying in a flashpacker hostel. It also means that even if you're legless, witless and brainless, and you find yourself regaining consciousness in a gutter at four a.m., the key to your room is resting against your chest. And hopefully it's vomit-free.

Gilligan's was most definitely a lanyard and swipe card kind of place. In fact, it seemed to be the gleaming future of backpacking. Outside was a big neon sign with iridescent palm trees surrounding the name—whoever oversees the estate of the late Sherwood Schwartz, who created *Gilligan's Island* (*Two Gilligan's Island references down, one to go*), would be well advised to have a look at it, as it bears a striking resemblance to the TV show's logo.

The reception area was all polished wood, glass and flatscreen TVs. Not only were there elevators going up to the rooms, but they appeared to work.

'You're checking in?' asked one of the girls behind the reception desk. 'Awesome, mate. Awesome.'

Awesome? This was the first time my mere decision to turn up at a backpackers hostel and deign to give them my custom was considered something to celebrate. The girl chewed furiously on some gum as she tapped away on the computer keyboard in front of her.

'Oh my God!' she exclaimed, pointing one finger up to the ceiling. 'I love this song!'

From the speaker system wafted some acoustic guitar and an easy, loping rhythm. I listened for a moment and then realised who it was. My old nemesis, Jack Johnson. The receptionist closed her eyes and started singing along. I smiled tightly, as you do when someone looks embarrassing. I was also hoping to god she wouldn't ask me my opinion of the music.

'Don't you just love this song?' she asked.

I thought about just nodding. Or lying and saying it was all right. And then I thought I should just be honest.

'You know what? I've been travelling up the east coast of Australia for over three weeks now. And from Bondi to

Byron Bay to Hervey Bay to Fraser Island to Airlie Beach to the Whitsundays to here, do you know what music plagued me constantly? Apart from the Scissor Sisters' 'I Don't Feel Like Dancing'. I'll tell you. Jack fucking Johnson. Look, I know his music is meant to be relaxing and laidback and goddamn smooth, but you know what? It's too polite. It's too pleasant. It's too goddamn smug. And it's everywhere. I mean, I have nothing against Jack personally. I'm sure he's a lovely guy who is a fine husband and father and all his mates think he's a good bloke. But why does he have to be there in every single fucking place I go on the eastern seaboard? Well? You can't tell me, can you? So in answer to your question, no. I don't love this song. I think it's beige-coloured background music, and it makes me want to strip naked, run into the jungle with Ted Nugent turned up to maximum volume on my iPod and scream at the top of my lungs that I'm not going to take it anymore!'

Of course, I didn't say that.

I nodded and said that I supposed the song was okay. And she gave me my swipe card on the end of an orange lanyard and wished me an awesome evening.

The elevator did indeed work and deposited me on the second floor. I walked past a large kitchen that had stoves in brushed steel, and multiple microwaves and large fridges with glass doors. Then I swiped open the door to my room, and although it was still just four double-decker bunks in a room, there was a modern, hotel-standard shower and separate toilet, and a large, airy balcony.

And there was Jack, an Englishman who turned 19 that day. He offered me a piece of his birthday cake, which was chocolate and had an illustration of the Bratz dolls in icing on top.

He arrived in Australia five weeks ago, and said he'd been drinking constantly since then. He was really feeling it at that moment because he and his buddy Adam were at the tail end of a five-day diving course, so instead of their regular schedule of partying and sleeping, they had to be up early every morning, doing a lot of study and spending hours underwater wearing heavy oxygen tanks.

After Australia they were going to New Zealand, where they would spend five months as pool guards and sports assistants at a school. Then they'd head home via Fiji, and perhaps Brazil and Argentina.

He'd just dropped into our room to pick up his iPod and invited me to come over to a room across the hall later if I wanted to hang out with him and his friends. I felt like crashing, but instead hit the shower and went out to eat first, then returned with some beer to room 233.

Inside, Jack and his friends were playing a drinking game that involved not being allowed to swear or say the word 'drinking'. Playing cards were also involved.

This group had met on Fraser Island a couple of weeks ago and had been crossing paths on the east coast trail ever since. English sisters Steph and Meg were sitting on one bunk with Jack's friend Adam. On the bunk opposite I was sitting with Jack and a Scottish girl called Vicki.

'Watch out for Vicki,' Adam announced. 'She's a cocktease. She has a boyfriend back at home.'

Vicki threw an empty plastic cup at him, and it bounced of his head with a satisfying popping noise.

I asked her how long she and her boyfriend had been together.

'Seven months,' she said.

'How come every girl I meet seems to have a boyfriend back at home who they've been with for seven months?' I said.

'That's true!' says Jack. 'It's a conspiracy!'

'Why don't you tell Barry all about your new girlfriend, Adam?' Vicki asks.

It turned out that Adam had sex with an American girl the night before. Everyone had been giving him a hard time about it ever since because the girl was 'a skank' and the deed was done in one of the sisters' beds while the rest of the group was still out partying.

The group drank steadily from a couple of casks of goon. They reminisced about their travels together. They took photos of each other. The girls discussed who had kissed another girl and who hadn't, and what exactly constituted a real kiss between girls anyway. The guys didn't discourage them from discussing this topic.

At around eleven o'clock everyone decided to go out to The Woolshed, a large club around the corner from the hostel. The Woolshed is also known as The Pull Shed. It's renowned as one of the biggest pick-up joints in the country, and its nickname comes from the claim that if you can't pull there, you can't pull anywhere.

As we walked from the lift and the airconditioned foyer out onto the street, we were hit with the heat and humidity of late night Cairns. It had rained earlier, and the street was slick. From the nightclub attached to Gilligan's, a muffled thumping beat and stuttering bass line reached the pavement, getting louder and then softer again as the doors opened and closed. We walked a couple of blocks down to the pedestrian mall of Shields Street, passing groups of revelling backpackers on their way between bars. Sitting on a bench just near The Woolshed, a girl was crying as she spoke loudly into her mobile phone. The person on the other end was apparently named Simon, and he was not in the good books at that moment.

It was hot and humid outside, but once inside the doors of The Woolshed, the temperature went up again. The air was moist, and it smelled of sweat and alcohol and hormones. Up onstage were two girls with no tops on. One had the Swedish flag painted across her breasts; the other had the American flag painted across hers. It was a Babe Nation contest, and we were witnessing the final.

'Which one of these lovely ladies will be the winner tonight?' the MC yelled into the microphone. 'It's up to you! Make some noise if you want Miss Sweden!'

Drinks were held aloft and the crowd made a noise like a herd of inebriated water buffalo.

'All right!' said the MC. 'Now make some noise if you want Miss USA!'

Drinks were held aloft and the crowd made a noise like a herd of inebriated water buffalo.

It looked like we had a tie.

'It looks like we've got a tie!' yelled the MC.

I was mildly horrified that my thoughts were in sync with a pub MC.

'Looks like we need a tie-breaker!' he added.

Imaginatively the tie-breaker involved the two girls being required to fondle and kiss each other for 60 seconds, which they proceeded to do with a minimum of fuss.

Of course, this was no way to decide a tie-breaker. How could one tell who was the winner? Tossing a coin or undertaking a game of rock paper scissors would have been more decisive. But getting a decision was not the point. Titillating the crowd and keeping people in the pub was the point.

To the surprise of no one, it was a dead heat. Everyone's a winner.

I noticed Jack giving Adam a hard time. He was nudging him in the rubs and rubbing the top of his head and laughing. So I asked what was going on.

'See Miss USA?' said Jack, trying to contain his laughter. 'That's the girl he shagged last night.'

Graham Smart is a veteran. He did five seasons on the Greek Islands, six seasons in Surfers Paradise and a season in Cancun, Mexico. He's a bachelor of bacchanalia, a dean of debauchery.

Not that he'd tell you this. He's a friendly, unassuming guy with a laidback demeanour and a bit of a gleam in his eye. But his job is to ferry people on a bus between drinking establishments and organise activities that will result in them getting lubricated, losing inhibitions and possibly getting laid.

'I've been doing this for seven years up here, and I've never had anybody throw up in the bus,' he said with some pride. 'And in 13 years of doing this around the world, there's never been one fight.'

What was his secret?

'Keep the guys and girls at a 50/50 ratio and everybody's happy.'

At the first bar on the schedule there's a game called nuts and bolts, a classic 'getting to know you' gambit. With an admirably blunt symbolism, each guy is given a bolt, each girl is given a nut, and they have to find the person with the bit of hardware that fits theirs. Graham claims that this game is so effective in getting people acquainted, that he knows of six couples who have gone on to get married after meeting up this way. One can only marvel at the story these people will tell their kids when they're asked the immortal question, 'How did you meet Mum, Dad?'

'Well, son, we were both paralytic up in Cairns, and my bolt fit her nut perfectly, so we won a white-water rafting trip. But we were too hungover to go, so we stayed in bed instead. And that's how you were made.'

Graham was at pains to point out that his patrons were fed twice during the evening.

'We start off with a light meal to line their stomachs. And three hours later we have pizza. So you see, we do look after them.'

The second stop featured a game where the guys sat on a chair with an air pump between their legs and a condom over the air nozzle. The girls then have to sit on top of the pump on the guys' laps and bounce up and down to inflate the condom. Suggestive!

'It's cheesy,' admitted Graham. 'But not sleazy.'

At the next bar it's time for the bubble gum game where the girls have to manually pass a piece of bubble gum up the inside of a guy's pants leg, across the top of his waist and back down the other leg, then chew the gum and blow a bubble. First bubble gets a prize. Tasty!

Back on the bus, then a new bar, a new game—Knights, Cavaliers, Vikings. This is like a drunker, more hands-on version of Simon Says. The call 'Knights!' means the girl has to sit on the guy's lap. 'Cavaliers!' means he lifts her up in his arms. 'Vikings!' means she jumps on his back. Educational!

At the last port of call, it's the When Harry Met Sally competition, which is basically a fake orgasm contest.

'No one's really shy at this point of the night,' Graham tells me, with some understatement.

Indeed, many of the women take to the microphone with gusto, and their performances surely make some of the men in the audience question their own sexual adequacy. And just to prove it's not simply a young person's game, tonight's winner is a 63-year-old, who puts on such a show that the club's staff all stand on top of the bar and applaud.

For their $25, these backpackers get a bit to eat, they get transported between places, and they get a chance to win prizes (reef trips, rafting trips, free restaurant meals). But of course, they're bringing in the bucks to the establishments along Graham's route, and it's basically a more ordered way to get drunk and pick up than just heading out to PJ O'Brien's and The Woolshed under your own steam with your mates and trying your luck. With Cairns's reputation as a good-time town and the renowned frugal (read: stingy) nature of many backpackers, $25 can be a tough sell.

'Cairns used to be a *real* party city,' said Graham. 'It's gotten quieter. The cyclone in 2006 affected the backpacker industry, licensing has cracked down on free drinks and promotions, and the council has cracked down on touts, so they've cleaned up the city a lot, but it's also taken away a bit of its character.

'I loved the old days, mate. You got away with a lot more back then.'

And presumably one didn't need a bus and a series of contrived games to get away with it.

Tony Soprano's guys had strip joint Bada Bing as their de facto office/boys club. The blokes who I came to regard as the Cairns mafia hung out at tables outside the Pomodoro café, at the entrance to Gilligan's.

As far as I know, they don't leave horse heads in their enemies' beds, nor do they fit them out with cement boots and take them for a long swim. But they do have a certain swagger, a boisterous camaraderie, and their fingers in enough local pies to make them seem, if not made guys, then self-made guys.

They also know Cairns and what makes it tick because that's their job. They've each found gaps in the market, or created a gap in the market, and rushed in to fill it. And they all rely on backpackers. Or, as they refer to them, flashpackers.

'We did a backpacker survey here about six months ago,' said Lance Collyer, the marketing manager for Gilligan's. 'The majority of them had one or two credit cards, big credit limits and a lot of parental backing.

'Twenty years ago a backpacker was someone who maybe didn't get on with their folks and left their family to travel the world and live on a shoestring. Not now. Look at that tour desk over there.'

To our right was a large tourist centre where the day before I'd booked trips to the Great Barrier Reef and Cape Tribulation.

'That's one of the busiest tour booking desks in the country, and it's attached to our hostel, which is one of the biggest hostels in the southern hemisphere. Five-hundred and forty beds, four floors, restaurants, pool, a nightclub that holds 1700 people.

'Backpackers are here to have a good time, and here they can do that without leaving the place, and then they can just go upstairs and fall into bed. That romantic old idea of backpacking has gone. It's a business now, it's more organised, and there's more money.'

Lance said this with a strange mixture of sadness and satisfaction. He obviously profited from the fact that backpackers were no longer scruffy hippies with no money, and the establishment for which he worked was designed to cater to these more cashed-up travellers, but at the same time he seemed to almost lament the old days of the adventure traveller. The backpacker was dead. Long live the flashpacker.

Ben Newman, who flashed a gold tooth in his smile as he shook my hand, first came to Australia in 1989 as an English backpacker. People told him that Cairns was a rubbish place to visit and it always rained. Being someone who never listened to what people told him, he bought a camper van in Kings Cross, made his way up here, and never left.

As more guys started attaching themselves to our table outside the café and started singing each others' praises, it emerged that Newman was responsible for much of the town's backpacker infrastructure. After working at the local newspaper, he started a backpacker magazine, and the others also 'credit' him with introducing Pole Idol, Babe Nation and Coyote Uglys, pub nights that mainly involved regular women acting like strippers. He used to own both the two café/restaurants in the Gilligan's complex and now owns a chain of petrol stations and a microbrewery.

None of these guys could easily fit everything they do on a business card. After a little head-scratching, Newman told me to refer to him as a publisher-turned-brewer. When he found out that I did a lot of music writing, he was also very keen to fill me in on another pet project—he was managing a girl group in Sydney. It seemed to be a town for entrepreneurs with a cowboy attitude and a desire to diversify and to party.

Which brings us to Ben Le-Van, who bought the two café/restaurants from Ben Newman. Le-Van was 29, he was originally from Sydney and he was not going back.

'Up here, backpackers don't differentiate between weeknights and weekends,' he said. 'Every night is Saturday night in Cairns. You've got to love a place like that.'

Le-Van was gregarious and likeable, and seemed to be the social centre of the group. He also coughed up his guts at 10-minute intervals and seemed to be recovering from a massive hangover. At one point he showed me dozens of the pictures on his camera—there were 497 on there, and the majority are of attractive girls from different countries. Le-Van said I should refer to him as a businessman who runs restaurants and does some trading at night. He was a smooth and somewhat manic character, who proved to be a cheerleader for Cairns. *(Full disclosure: he insisted on putting a couple of meals I ate with him on his tab, and didn't like seeing me or my new friends—especially my attractive Swiss friends Sabrina and Martina—with an empty glass in our hands.)*

He also big-noted his buddies, something which all of these guys did, and which lent them a further comparison with wiseguys. There was much friendly ribbing and backslapping. Le-Van introduced me to Anthony Brooks and said I simply must talk to him. Anthony was 36, had thick, curly, greying hair, and spoke quietly and intently. He opened Gilligan's in late 2003, and is the managing director.

'No one was spending money up here because of the airline crisis at the time,' he said, referring to the collapse of Ansett in 2001. 'But this is a great town, it attracts a lot of young people, and we saw an opportunity. No one had ever done a premium backpackers, a more upmarket place that has everything they need under one roof.'

Just then Chopper walked up and said hello. Not *the* Chopper—the notorious Australian droopy-moustached, earless underworld figure. The Cairns Chopper—whose mother knew him as Fabio—had both his ears. He was moustachioed, built like an outdoor toilet block, and got the blessing of the real Chopper Read to continue to use his nickname. Fabio was hired as Read's security man when he was touring Queensland as a double-act with former footballer Mark 'Jacko' Jackson (who was famous for 15 minutes in the 1980s for saying 'oi!', releasing a single called 'I'm An Individual' and appearing in TV advertisements for batteries).

'Chopper's a really nice bloke,' said Fabio, although it's rare to find someone who says that Chopper Read is anything other than a total gent, especially if those people have seen Eric Bana's portrayal of the aforementioned total gent in the movie *Chopper*.

The Cairns Chopper was 41 years old and had worked the door at O'Brien's and The Woolshed for the last five years.

Although he agreed that backpackers were much more cashed-up than they used to be, he reckoned they were still cheap and stingy, complaining about a six-dollar entry fee to a nightclub and expecting free drink deals wherever they went. Although he'd had trouble with tourists, he maintained that locals caused most of the problems in Cairns.

'I've got to say that I understand where they're coming from,' he said. 'They feel like they're being squeezed out of their own place, and they don't like it. Just about everywhere around here caters for backpackers.'

Fabio could pinpoint the biggest problem he faced as a doorman in Cairns.

'The three o'clock lockout,' he said. 'It's the worst thing that happened to this town. With the places that have a five o'clock licence, there's a three o'clock lockout, where if you're not in there by three, then you can't get in. The people outside don't want to go home, everyone else is in there having a good time, and things get ugly. You can get 60 or 70 people out there arguing with you. It can be real shitfight.'

Anthony, a wiry little guy who was head chef at a local restaurant came up to the group and exchanged hellos with everyone.

'Look at the time!' he said. 'It's three in the afternoon already! It's beer o'clock! Let's get out of here!'

It looked like business was done for the day. Until tonight, anyway.

*   *   *

Cairns used to be a swamp. I'm not putting it down by saying that. It quite literally was a swamp. In the late 1800s, the town's forefathers started clearing the mangroves and filling the marshy ground with sawdust, dried mud, and rock and debris from a nearby quarry. Cairns was built on crap.

I was thinking about this fact as I strolled along the Esplanade, a waterside walkway that is the pride of the city. Families ambled by holding ice-creams; roller-bladers and joggers braved the heat; a couple of Japanese tourists asked me to take a photo of them. Pelicans glided in to land on the shallow water. I passed a war memorial whose clock had its hands painted permanently at 4:28—was this representative of the eternal 'beer o'clock' Cairns seemed to inhabit?

Despite being the gateway to the Great Barrier Reef, and despite postcards of the area depicting idyllic pictures of the clear water, exotic fish and magnificent coral, you couldn't actually swim anywhere around here. The 'beach' is a vast stretch of mud flats ringed with mangroves swamps. You wouldn't jump in there if the water was dotted with beckoning mermaids serving free beer.

Seven years ago it was decided that something had to be done about this, and once I got to the end of The Esplanade, I saw what it was. Just like in Airlie Beach, they had built a landscaped swimming pool, and called it a lagoon. Here it was, packed with swimmers and sunbathers, stretching across 4 hectares of waterfront land. Sticking out of the water were poles that stretched into the air and supported modernist metallic sculptures of fish. It cost $24 million, but everyone in the tourism industry in Cairns thinks it was worth every cent, as the only things that want to get their feet wet in the water offshore are those pelicans.

I got talking to the security guard on duty. His name was James, but he told me to call him Irish, not the most imaginative nickname for someone of Irish heritage.

'The lagoon really changed Cairns,' he said. 'Five or six years ago there'd be 30 parkies *(homeless people)* hanging on that wall over there. A lot of public drunkenness during the day. That's changed. Things change every six months up here. A lot's happening all the time.'

It turned out that just like in Airlie, the lagoon was a magnet for backpackers wanting to indulge in nocturnal aquatic activities.

'Between about two and five in the morning we get what you would expect,' said Irish. 'Drunk people wanting to dive in here, drunk people wanting to drink in here, and drunk people wanting to have sex in here.'

Australia's federal treasurer Peter Costello famously said in 2006 that our country needed to make more babies.

'Have one for mum, one for dad, and one for the country,' he said, before flashing the idiotic grin he is famous for.

If Mr Costello ever becomes Prime Minister, here's my suggestion for his 'procreate or perish' policy—build more man-made lagoons. Or as he can rebrand them, spawning grounds.

I waded back through the oppressively humid streets to the hostel, and sitting at a table at the café outside were

Jack and Adam, who I hadn't even heard come in the night before.

'I was late, maybe four o'clock,' said Jack. 'Adam didn't come in at all.'

What happened with you, Adam?

'I hooked up with a bird from Basingstoke who we met in the Whitsundays. I didn't even think it was on. We'd all been doing shots at The Woolshed. I can't even remember how many because I lost count. First we just came back to the TV room and we dozed off. When I came to she basically said, 'Come over here.' It was all her. She took me back to her room and we did it with three other people in the room. I was a bit worried the old didgeridoo wouldn't work. Then right afterwards she says, "My boyfriend won't like this." I'm thinking, "Why the fuck did she say that?"'

Better to say it after than before, I suppose.

'I guess so,' said Adam.

'So you've had sex with two different women in two days,' Jack said to his friend.

'Yeah,' said Adam. 'Not bad I suppose. But no Wills.'

'Who's Wills?' I asked.

'He's this guy we know who had three Brazilians in one night,' said Jack. 'It was two sisters and their cousin. Bang, bang, bang.'

'The next night he got off with a Canadian, but the didgeridoo wouldn't work,' Adam chimed in. 'But I don't think he really cared too much at that point.'

'You're up for your hat-trick tonight, mate,' Jack said to Adam, poking him in the ribs.

The next morning, their last in Cairns, they informed me that Adam didn't get the hat-trick.

Jack, however, got lucky.

Where?

The lagoon, of course.

The first British backpacker to come to Australia, hang around for ages, and complain about it, was back in 1770. His name was James Cook. He was a lieutenant in the British Navy, but on his return to the old country, everyone was so impressed with his discoveries and his stories, and the pictures his naturalists drew of the crazy wildlife over here, that they eventually made him a captain.

Cook didn't have a great time in northern Queensland. You can tell by the names he gave places up here—Mount Warning, Weary Bay, Mount Sorry, Cape Tribulation.

Yes, Cooksy—as no one but me ever called him—was the first whingeing Pom. Although, to be fair, unlike his countrymen from a couple of centuries later, who bitch about our fair country when they come from bad weather, worse food and a favourable exchange rate that means they can live like royalty here even if they lived in a squat in Bradford back at home, he had pretty good reason to complain by the time he got this far up the eastern coastline.

His ship, *Endeavour*, hit a reef, the coral made a very large, inconvenient gash in the hull, the boat was taking in more water than the crew could pump back out, and it seriously looked like it was going to break up and sink. If things had gone differently he not only wouldn't have been promoted to captain, he would have been shark food.

But due to an ingenious—and apparently non-sexual—procedure called fothering (where a sail was basically wrapped under the hull and utilised as 1770's biggest bandage) *Endeavour* did not meet the same fate as the SS *Minnow*, and unlike the Skipper and Gilligan (—*and that's the last Gilligan's Island reference, I promise)*, Cook and his crew did not have to spend three TV seasons stranded on an island in the middle of nowhere with a movie star (which, let's face it, would have been ridiculous, as movie stars hadn't even been invented in 1770).

Cook and his crew ate more healthily than English backpackers of today, too, even though he was here over 200 years before there was a decent Thai restaurant in Australia. One thing that every primary school kid in Australia learned was that Cook managed to prevent his crew from dying of scurvy (a rampant disease among sailors of the time caused by a lack of vitamin C) by making them eat sauerkraut and drink lemon or lime juice. If Cook had been discovering Australia in 2007, of course, there'd be nothing on the menu but instant noodles.

By the way, the main purpose of Cook's trip wasn't actually to discover a brand new country that could beat

England at cricket, but to go to Tahiti and observe the transit of the planet Venus across the face of the sun. He apparently achieved this without ingesting any ecstasy. If he had, he could have spared himself the trouble of an almost three-year ocean voyage and just gone to a rave at home in Plymouth and seen the same thing.

After *Endeavour* was mended and made it to the northerly tip of Australia at Cape York, Cook landed on an island, named it Possession Island, and planted a Union Jack on a pole in the soil. We still haven't managed to get the thing out of the upper left-hand corner of our own flag. Yet.

I was thinking about Cook because we'd just passed another Big Thing. Yes, it was the Big Captain Cook, a stiff-looking statue standing on the outskirts of Cairns. I know it sounds strange to call a statue stiff-looking, but if this monument is an accurate depiction of the real Cook, then he had the most exemplary posture of any man in history, he was unfeasibly skinny even for a man who survived at sea for long stretches, and if the legs of the 7-metre high effigy are to scale, then he could have been the Michael Jordan of his day.

'See how he's holding his arm out straight like that?' asked Wayne, our driver and tour guide. 'That's to show how high the marijuana plants grow around here.'

I smiled and wrote this down. The pale English girl up the back maintained her grumpy countenance. The Chinese guy and his Japanese girlfriend didn't appear to know what Wayne was talking about. It was just the four of us, heading north to the Daintree Rainforest and Cape Tribulation in a four-wheel drive. A little later we passed a golf course that had a replica of the bridge at the famous St Andrews course in Scotland. The only difference is that they claim the one here is bigger.

As Wayne was a tour guide, he was laconic and well-stocked with wisecracks. He was also not afraid to be politically incorrect, joking that Kuranda (a rainforest town in the hinterland north-west of Cairns) is an Aboriginal word for 'tourist rip-off', and that a local beach favoured by the gay community is nicknamed Ashtray Bay (because it's full of fags). He also informed us that barramundi are all male when they're born, but later change their sex.

'It must be confusing,' he told us. 'One day you're hanging out with your mates, doing the things mates do together. Then the next day your mates start changing into girls.'

Wayne then told us he'd be cooking us lunch later in the day, and that we had a choice of steak, vegetarian, or barramundi. I chose the barramundi. It would be the first time I'd be eating the fish knowing that I was devouring a transsexual.

Less than half an hour later we were driving through Palm Cove. There's something not quite right with the palm trees in Palm Cove. They have no coconuts in them. Wayne told us that the resort town actually hires people to regularly 'de-nut' the trees. In this marvellous 21st century we live in, the possibility of a stray coconut falling from some height and hitting a tourist on his or her litigious head is just too great a risk to take.

When the sun hits Palm Cove at the right angle, it certainly has natural beauty, but it's also something of a Stepford-ish kind of place. It was the inaugural winner of the Australia's Cleanest Beach award, and it advertises itself as Australia's number one destination for spas and weddings. Even the *Lonely Planet* calls it 'the glamourpuss of Cairns' northern beaches' and adds that it 'encourages idleness and indulgence'.

As well as keeping its visitors free from contact with hard round objects lurking in trees, some Palm Cove resorts have penthouse suites that cost as much for a weekend as I spent in my entire month away, and they use Rolls Royces as courtesy cars to ferry their guests to and from the airport.

Just off the coast, Wayne pointed out two large, rounded bits of land that poked up through the water—the locals sometimes refer to it as Dolly Parton Island. It's real name is Double Island, and you will never stay there. That's being presumptuous, I know, but it's renowned as possibly the most expensive resort in all of Australia.

Welcome to paradise, as scripted by Aaron Spelling or Donald Trump. Or Christopher Skase.

Skase is one of two famous Australians who met a spectacular end in far north Queensland. As Wayne pulled the four-wheel drive into Port Douglas, we could see the spot where Skase met his end figuratively; off the coast, Wayne pointed out where Steve Irwin met his literally.

Most backpackers know all about Irwin. Even the Japanese girl on our tour, who didn't appear to follow too much of what was going on, perked up and said 'crocodile man!' when Wayne mentioned his name. But no one recognised Skase's name.

Way back in a magical faraway time known as the 1980s, Christopher Skase lived such a fairytale life that he was even married to a woman named Pixie. He put the town of Port Douglas, 70 kilometres north of Cairns, on the map as a tourist destination thanks to a resort called the Mirage.

Queensland entrepreneurs in the 1980s were known as the white shoe brigade, and Skase was the Imelda Marcos of the bunch. It was rumoured that one Christmas party he held cost almost half a million dollars (and remember, this was over 20 years ago), and stories abounded of his excesses, such as ordering his pilot to fly his private jet from Port Douglas to Melbourne and back just to pick up a particular dress that his wife wanted.

If you can judge a man by the men he admires, then perhaps we can judge Skase by his admiration of Sir Joh Bjelke-Petersen, the man who ruled Queensland from 1968 to 1987. Bjelke-Petersen allowed rampant corruption, fostered over-development, and restricted civil liberties. (Queensland also steadfastly decided against changing to daylight saving time each year, when all the other eastern states went ahead. To this day, from October to March, Queensland is an hour behind New South Wales, Victoria,

Tasmania and the ACT. Some would say that the state lags much further behind than just 60 minutes.)

Skase had nothing but good things to say about Sir Joh. He considered him on par with Australia's longest serving Prime Minister, Sir Robert Menzies, and once said he was 'one of the two greatest politicians and political leaders and managers that this country has ever seen'. He also once equated Paul Keating with Hitler, a comparison that even John Howard, Keating's old nemesis, would baulk at.

Prophetically, Skase's company's advertising used the tagline 'too good to be true'. And Mirage proved to be an appropriate name for his luxury resorts, because eventually the money started to become as tangible as a shimmery desert vision. As the 1980s ended, so did the fairytale. Skase made a bid for MGM studios in Hollywood, the financing collapsed, and the 1989 pilot strike proved fatal for his resorts. He declared bankruptcy two years later, with personal debts of $80 million and corporate debts of $1.5 billion. He claimed he only had $170 in the bank, despite the fact he'd been claiming millions of dollars in management fees as his company was imploding.

And then he scarpered, flying to the Spanish island of Majorca. Over the next decade, the Australian government tried to have him extradited, but he claimed he couldn't return because of health problems. The efforts to get him back became known as The Chase For Skase. When he appeared in public at one point sitting in a wheelchair and wearing an oxygen mask, it provided rich material for satirists, comedians, cartoonists and angry letter writers for some time. In 1998, the government cancelled his Australian passport so he became a citizen of Dominica. They never succeeded in making him face charges as Skase died in August 2001 of stomach cancer and a lung tumour.

Although Irwin was also sent-up by comedians and satirists, the reaction to his death was an unprecedented groundswell of sorrow. He was the Crocodile Hunter, and he was considered a bit of a throwback to the ocker boofhead stereotype of *Crocodile Dundee* when he emerged to mainstream popularity in the 1990s. In fact, he was much more popular in the United States than his own country, and his documentaries and TV specials often involved him annoying animals and exclaiming 'crikey!' when they snapped at him.

On 4 September 2006, while filming on the reef for one of his TV documentaries, he was speared in the chest by a stingray's tail. He pulled the barb out, and died of a heart attack. The public reaction really surprised a cynic like myself. Even before a naysayer could scoff at the announcement that the Irwin family had been offered a state funeral, they politely turned it down, claiming Irwin wouldn't have wanted such a fuss made over his passing. With that said, a memorial service held a couple of weeks later at Irwin's Australia Zoo was televised live and commercial-free on three of the five Australian free-to-air networks, as if it was a day of national mourning.

Both Skase and Irwin were genuine Queensland stereotypes, a guy who was a big spender, and a guy who was a big larrikin. In death, even bad guys often get some kudos, but to the general public and the media, Skase remained a crook, a scoundrel, a coward and a bit of a wanker. Irwin, on the other hand, was elevated as a colourful enthusiast for the environment, and was tagged with that most Australian of compliments, a good bloke. Although if crocodiles could dial telephones and call in to talkback shows, one wonders if they would have been so glowing about a man who insisted on grabbing their tails, pulling faces and yelling a lot.

'Choose a seat without teeth marks in it,' warned Wayne as he sent us on our way down to the boat that was to take us along the Daintree River.

'Choose a seat without teeth marks on it,' said a driver with another group as we waited at the jetty.

'Choose a seat without teeth marks on it,' said our boat captain when we climbed aboard.

They really needed to coordinate their routine a little better and come up with a few more jokes. I suspected we would be offered the chance to buy T-shirts with that phrase emblazoned across the front at the end of our tour.

Our boat captain's name was Bill. As he was a boat captain, Bill was laconic and well-stocked with wisecracks. He spent a large portion of our time on the Daintree River informing us of the many and varied ways to be maimed or killed in the area.

The most obvious, and perhaps most unimaginative way to shuffle of your mortal coil around here is to be eaten by a crocodile. If they don't get you, there's always the snakes. Even the stuff that doesn't swim or slither can cause you some bother. Some of the mangroves that line the Daintree contain a sap that spits out if the branches get broken, and can blind you.

'Worst case scenario,' said Bill. 'You get attacked by a crocodile, so you climb a mangrove with your one good arm. There's a snake in the mangrove that bites you on the other arm, so you fall out of the mangrove and on the way down you snap some branches that spit sap in your eye and blind you. And then you fall in the water and get run over by a train.'

He pointed up the river, and sure enough, a boat that was done up like a train engine with a series of carriages was chugging towards us.

He also informed us that the 1996 movie *The Phantom,* starring Billy Zane, was filmed up here, and pointed out the peak that was used to represent Skull Mountain, the home of The Ghost Who Walks. So worse things could happen to you than Captain Bill's horror scenario. The poison sap mightn't completely blind you, and you could feasibly still see *The Phantom,* which, apart from Halle Berry's 2004 dog *Catwoman,* is possibly the worst superhero movie ever made.

Two years after *The Phantom,* according to Bill, a call went out to locals who had been on the dole for at least six months. They were 'drafted' into appearing as extras in *The*

Thin Red Line, the WWII film directed by Terence Malick. Along with the actors, including Sean Penn, John Travolta, Nick Nolte, Woody Harrelson, Adrien Brody and John C. Reilly, they underwent a two-week boot camp under a former Vietnam veteran. They were paid $130 a day and had to get a short back and sides haircut once a week. Which just goes to show what a magical place northern Queensland is. If you hang around long enough, and if the crocs, snakes, spitting mangroves, boat trains and job market don't get you, Hollywood stardom awaits.

Our boat, which was basically a long aluminium 'tinny' with bench seats and a canopy for shade, slowly buzzed along the winding river, and Bill told us to keep our eyes peeled for shapes in the water that could be crocodiles. There were many false alarms, which turned out to be floating logs.

On one side of the river, Bill cut the engine and pointed out hundreds of black objects hanging from the trees along the bank. Then one moved, unfurled its wings and flew to another tree. They were bats. We looked at them for a few minutes and then Bill quietly said, 'Ah, look at this. Someone wants some lunch.'

He was a low-tech kind of guy and took a small mirror from his pocket, angling it towards the sun so a beam of light stretched into the trees.

'See him?' he asked.

We strained our eyes and sure enough, well camouflaged and moving stealthily along a branch, was a snake. He was closing in on a dozing bat which was hanging upside-down just 5 metres away. But the frantic squeaks of other nearby bats roused their unwitting friend, and he flew to another tree before the snake could strike.

After an hour, we still hadn't seen a crocodile, and our tour was almost over. But just 10 minutes from disembarking, Bill spotted something hiding in the mangroves. He pulled up to within a few metres of the bank, and through the tangled roots we saw a croc called Scoot. He earned his name from the fact that he's missing one of his scoots, which are the bumpy ridges along a crocodile's tail.

Scoot's scoot was removed by National Parks and Wildlife for study and to ascertain how old he was. By taking a cross section, much like counting the rings in a tree trunk, they estimated that he was six years and ten months old. Bill wasn't a big fan of National Parks and Wildlife, and made this known to us. He made grumbling noises about the way they came up here like they owned the place, and said that they should just leave the local wildlife alone to get on with being wildlife.

'I told them to piss off,' he says of those that took Scoot's scoot. According to Bill, they haven't scooted back since.

Back on dry land, we re-united with Wayne and hopped back into the four-wheel drive, plunging further north into the forest towards Cape Tribulation. The tree canopy closed in around us, and we passed yellow signs that displayed the black outline of a bird. This was the cassowary, a flightless bird that looks like a cross between an emu and a drag queen. It has a long blue neck, a horn-like crest on top of its head, can reach almost 2 metres in height, and run up to 50 kilometres an hour. The signs were to warn drivers that cassowaries could be crossing the road, so they should take care, as they're an endangered species. Wayne added that if the birds are distressed, provoked or threatened, they can disembowel you with a flash of the long sharp middle claw on each of their feet. So maybe the signs were protecting us from them as much as the other way around.

A half hour later we stopped for lunch at a place crawling with thousands of creepy-crawlies. Well, not literally crawling with creepy-crawlies, because most of them were dead and had a pin stuck through their middle.

It was the Daintree Entomological Museum, inland from Thornton Beach, which is about halfway between the Daintree River and Cape Tribulation. After passing through the gates that were fashioned to look like big spider webs, we entered a building that was filled with case after case of everything from butterflies to bees to cicadas to moths. Some of the beetles were as big as birds. The woman who was running the place informed us in hushed tones that the owner, Stephen Lamond, had been collecting for over 30 years, had amassed over 150,000 specimens, and had even discovered a few new species of beetle, one of which he named after his wife, which I hope she appreciated. She asked us if we'd like to hold a leaf insect, and unsurprisingly no one volunteered.

She'd been living out here since the 1970s, but told me she was about to move. I imagined that after that long surrounded by the makings of a horror movie, she was fine with the insects. Did the move have something to do with the fact that she was in the absolute middle of nowhere and was now craving a bit of hustle, a bit of bustle, some conversation, and a good coffee? No, it didn't.

'It's become too busy out here now,' she said, seriously. 'We get more and more tours out this way now, so I'm moving somewhere with a bit more peace and quiet.'

A bit more peace and quiet? I looked around at the kilometres of thick forest in every direction and wondered where on earth she would end up that could possibly be more remote than here. The Daintree made Hobart look like Delhi.

Wayne called us down to the creek that ran through the property, where he'd been cooking lunch on a barbecue. I'm not sure whether my barramundi had gone through a sex change yet, but it was delicious. As we ate, large, brilliantly coloured butterflies fluttered around us and we watched a couple of small turtles down at the edge of the creek. Yep, it certainly was hectic. If you lived around here you'd certainly want to get out and find a bit of peace and quiet.

Wayne had noticed I'd been taking notes, and asked me what I did for a living. When I told him I was a writer he quizzed me about whether I had any contacts in the film industry. He'd written a screenplay about backpackers. He explained that it was set in Western Australia. A motley bunch of travellers buy a clapped-out Kombi van, and while they're driving on a remote bit of highway, their world collides, quite literally, with a bikie gang whose members have just ripped off a fortune. When the dust settles after the crash, the backpackers are the last ones standing, and as dead bikies tell no tales, the backpackers decide to grab the loot and never tell anyone what happened. But, of course, one of the bikies isn't dead, so he sets off in pursuit.

It didn't sound like a bad concept at all, like a cross between *Duel, Mad Max* and *He Died With A Felafel In His Hand*. I suggested that if he threw in a rogue cassowary and a museum of dead insects that suddenly and inexplicably came to life, then his people could talk to my people. If I had any people.

On the way further north we stopped at a couple of rainforest walks. It had started to rain lightly, so Wayne provided us with umbrellas as we wandered on paths and boardwalks that cut through the bush. Wayne pointed out various plants—the strangler figs that dangled down from the tops of the tallest trees and wound around their trunks like thick ropes; the lawyer vine or wait-a-while, named because its barbs catch on your clothing as you walk through the rainforest, and you have to stop to disengage yourself. We saw a couple of goannas and also a brush turkey, and Wayne was able to locate its nest, a mound of earth around 3 metres across and over a metre high, that was made from moist dirt and decomposing leaves, and operated like an incubator for the bird's eggs.

The Dubiji Boardwalk, our final stop before Cape Tribulation, was also notable for some introduced species—Vashti, Emma and Mel, the three English girls I met on the boat in the Whitsundays, were just starting the walk as my group was returning. We agreed to meet up the following night, my final night of the trip.

From there it was a short drive to Cape Tribulation, and Wayne directed us to go it alone on foot through to the beach and onto the walkway out to the cape itself. The sun was only shining weakly through the threatening grey clouds, and the wind was starting to build, so the idyllic pictures you usually see of this part of the world didn't really match what we saw. But it was still impressive, a wide crescent of sand with the rainforest on one side of it and the Coral Sea on the other.

By the time we got to the end of the walkway and stood on the cape, it started to rain. And Jessica, the English girl, started to whine.

'Typical,' she said. 'I thought it wasn't meant to rain in this country. It never seems to stop up here.'

I explained that it was actually the wet season and we were in the tropics. What else had she been up to while she was here?

'I went white-water rafting yesterday.'

How was it?

'Terrible. I fell out and had to be pulled out of the water. It was a level four river. Do you believe it?'

I don't know. How high do the levels go?

'Only to six! Why were we on a level four when we were beginners? Now I've hurt my back. They said, 'It's strange, because no one's ever fallen out at that point in the river.' The only good thing that came out of it was that they got this big, good-looking Fijian guy to sit with me after that. He was gorgeous.'

Well that's something, then.

'It didn't make up for it, though. I went skydiving the day before that.'

I almost hesitated to ask, but did anyway. And did you enjoy that?

'No.'

Ooh, there's a surprise, I thought to myself.

'I'll never do that again. I wanted a guy to jump with me but instead I got a girl.'

Why was that a problem?

'Well, I didn't trust she was experienced enough, and I wanted someone big to hold onto me.'

This girl had a thing about big men, apparently.

It doesn't sound like you're having a very good time with all this adventure stuff, I ventured. Why are you putting yourself through it?

'I'm a bit of a wimp,' she finally admitted. 'I decided to do it all while I'm up here because I couldn't really do it at home. But I've got to go back to Sydney next week because I've got to get a job. It's expensive in Australia, isn't it?'

Oh fuck off, I thought to myself. And go back to sunny, cheap England, where everyone knows the beer's lovely and cold, the weather's dry and warm, and the girls are bronzed and beautiful.

Not long after I returned to Sydney, Mercer Human Resources Consulting published the results of their Worldwide Quality Of Living Survey.

Average price of a cup of coffee in Sydney? $3.30. In London? $4.71.

Average price of a hamburger meal in Sydney? $6.15. In London? $9.17.

Average price of a bus ride in Sydney? $2.38. In London? $7.07.

In fact, London was the second most expensive city on the planet behind Moscow. And overall, Sydney came in as the ninth most liveable city in the world when it came to quality of life. London came 39th.

If I'd only had these results a few months earlier, I could have got into a lot more arguments and been much more insufferable. And much more right.

It was already late in the afternoon, and the drive back to Cairns would take almost two hours. By the time we'd emerged from the rainforest and headed south again on the highway, Wayne's four passengers were dozing after a long day. He did wake me up just outside of Mossman, however. I'd noticed a shed on the way up, and Wayne thought I might like to have my photo taken next to it. I blearily made my way towards it, my feet sinking in wet grass and mud, and stood leaning against it while Wayne snapped away. In capital letters over a metre high someone had painted onto the corrugated iron: BAZ.

There are a number of things you could feasibly do while sitting on a high speed motorboat cruising its way to the Great Barrier Reef. You could, for instance, gaze out at a stretch of tropical water and ponder the fact that it contains the world's largest living thing, an ecosystem that is 2000 kilometres long and supports 1500 species of fish and 400 types of coral.

Or, you could sit with your partner and do a quiz from a book entitled *Why Marriages Succeed Or Fail*. The American couple opposite me choose to do exactly this.

The previous evening I'd re-united with my Swiss friends Martina and Sabrina, and my old English swimming buddy Jeff, and we'd been out until three in the morning, drinking and dancing at Gilligan's nightclub, then PJ O'Brien's. So I wasn't feeling a million bucks when I had to get up at seven o'clock the next morning to catch a bus to Port Douglas, retrace my route from the day before, then board a boat out to the reef. But here I was. With the American couple who were trying to re-evaluate their marriage.

He was square-jawed and had an intense stare and a certain nervous energy that was a little disconcerting. She had a bad perm, an intense stare and a certain nervous energy that was a little disconcerting. So apart from the perm and the square jaw, they appeared to be very well matched indeed.

They silently read a chapter of the book together. He read faster than she did and waited for her to get to the end of a page before asking, 'Ready, hon?' She would nod and smile nervously. He would turn the page and they would continue.

At the end of the chapter she ripped out two pieces of paper from her tiny notebook, and they did some sort of quiz relating to what they'd just read. Then they swapped their answers to see where they matched up and where they didn't.

Then they had an argument over what constitutes an argument. Seriously, they really did.

'When you correct me about something, how do you think I should react?' she asked. 'I have to say something, and if I disagree with what you're saying, that doesn't mean it's an argument.'

'What does it mean then, hon?' he asked.

'It means I'm expressing my opinion.'

'But one person expressing an opinion, and then the other person expressing an opposing opinion, by definition, is an argument.'

'No, it's a discussion.'

'Okay. Then when does a discussion become an argument?'

This was a very good question but I never found out the answer, as I quietly left my seat, went up on deck, made deep cuts into both my arms, and threw myself overboard to be taken by a school of sharks so I wouldn't have to listen to these people anymore.

But I kept thinking about them, especially when we finally got to the first of three reefs we were going to explore that day. Most of us had been fitted out with wetsuits, flippers, goggles and snorkels, but I noticed that the American couple were part of the small group who were going scuba diving. As I was floating in the warm, clear water adjusting my goggles, I saw them glide past me. The husband gave me a thumbs-up.

I was basically by myself, and went off snorkelling around the reef, gliding along the surface, following the nooks and crannies of the coral, hovering over any particularly vibrantly coloured or unusually shaped formations or fish.

After about 15 minutes of this, I poked my head back up out of the water and realised I'd drifted a fair distance from the boat, and there wasn't anyone else around. And that's when I remembered the story of the Lonergans, and did a U-turn.

Tom and Eileen Lonergan were a married couple from Louisiana who had been US Peace Corps teachers in Tuvalu and Fiji, and came to Australia for a holiday. On 25 January 1998, they'd taken a daytrip on the Reef. It was a trip very similar to the one I was on right now.

They never returned from the last dive of the day, but no one actually noticed this until 48 hours later, when a bag was found on board, and there were the Lonergans' passports and wallets inside. A search was undertaken, but it soon became obvious they weren't showing up, and most assumed that they'd stayed underwater too long, emerged to find the boat had gone, and died by drowning, dehydration or shark attack.

Fingers were pointed at the tour operator and crew for the lax measures they took when it came to headcounts and diving logs. (I did notice on our trip that there was an announcement over the loudspeaker before the boat took off at the end of each dive, telling us to freeze, so two crew members could make independent tallies of the people on board using clickers, to make sure everyone who jumped off was back on again.)

But soon the Lonergans' story got weirder. The couple's belongings were found at the hotel where they were staying, and their diaries made very interesting reading. Up to that point the Lonergans were portrayed as a happy loving couple, but their diaries revealed that they hated their jobs as teachers. Worse, in an entry just two weeks before they disappeared, Elaine had written that Tom had a death wish, and that 'I could get caught in that'. A few months earlier, her husband had written: 'I feel that my life is complete and I am ready to die'.

Still, it was argued that the diary excerpts read out at the inquest and the trial of the boat's captain were taken out of context. It was harder to explain what was washing up on the beaches, however. Items of the couple's gear, including flotation devices, air tanks and a vest with Tom's name on it, were found up to 100 kilometres away from where they disappeared, without any bite marks on them. It was pointed out by experienced divers that the two were not novices, and that there was a diving platform and an exposed reef not far away from where they were last seen, where they could have stayed until they were found.

Eerier stories started cropping up, of an unknown fishing boat that was seen speeding away just before the dive boat started its trip back to shore, and of numerous alleged sightings of the couple on the mainland in the days and weeks after the story broke. Rumours started to swirl about a suicide pact, a murder-suicide, or an intricate plan to completely disappear and start a new life.

Naturally, the parents of the couple scoffed at the rumours, claiming that it was the incompetence of the tour operators that resulted in the Lonergans being left behind to die. And naturally, it turned out many of the rumours and suggestions that the Lonergans had everything to do with their own disappearance were coming from the tour operators, as they didn't want bad press for an industry that generated around four and a half billion dollars a year.

Six months later, a fisherman found a dive slate—a board that can be written on in water—that was dated 26 January 1998. Someone had written that they were abandoned on Agincourt Reef the previous day, wrote the name of the boat that the Lonergans were on, and added 'Please help us. Rescue us before we die. Help!!!'

If you're thinking all of this sounds like it could be the stuff of a movie, then you're right. They ended up making one called *Open Water* in 2003, roughly based on the real story.

I made my way back towards the boat and started thinking about the American couple I'd met on board. What if they disappeared, just like the Lonergans, and I was questioned about them? I was sitting opposite them, and out of everyone on the boat, I would have been the one who knew the most about them.

'Think carefully,' a detective with a beer gut and a bad comb-over would tell me. 'Do you remember anything at all about what they were talking about while they were on the boat?'

'Well,' I would say, scratching the stubble on my chin, sipping a coffee, while dragging heavily on a cigarette. I'm not sure why I'm doing this, as I don't smoke, but I seem to be acting like a stereotypical witness in this scenario, so I'll just go with it.

'Well, I'm not sure if this means anything, but...'

'Yes?' asks the detective, raising an eyebrow.

'Well, I noticed they were reading a book and doing a quiz at the end of each chapter.'

'Do you have any recollection of the name of this book?'

'As a matter of fact I do.' I say, crushing the cigarette into an ashtray, and exhaling a plume of smoke. '*Why Marriages Succeed Or Fail.*'

Cue dramatic music.

Back in reality on board our boat, after a headcount and speeding our way to another reef, the wife talked about the mild panic attack she had under the water, while her husband nodded patiently and patted her hand. He reminded me of an ostrich, and she reminded me of a poodle.

After our third and final dive I was so exhausted that I laid out on my bench seat and promptly fell asleep, only coming to when I sensed the boat was slowing and we were coming in to dock.

I rubbed my eyes, and when I opened them the couple was looking at me.

'Well someone had a good nap,' said the wife, with a smile.

'We lost you for a while there,' said the husband. 'Good to have you back.'

I smiled back at them and was kind of glad that they didn't end up as the subject of a B-grade telemovie about their disappearance.

'I hope I didn't miss anything,' I said.

It was three o'clock in the morning—again—and I was standing in the middle of a street in Cairns, physically and emotionally drained, slightly drunk, and drenched to the bone.

The last eight hours had been a little like an episode of a TV show called *This Is Your Life (From The Last Four Weeks)*. Or like the final scenes of a movie, where a bunch of characters you've got to know all come in and out of the action in the closing minutes.

For me, the ant trail was coming to an end, and it seemed that every third person I'd met in the past month showed their face at some point throughout the night. The evening passed by in a series of snapshots, reminiscent of the dozens of times I'd sat with backpackers in bars, in buses, on bunks, on balconies and on beaches, as they'd scrolled through the pictures on their digital cameras.

* * *

Flash.

It's the beginning of the evening, I'm sitting in a booth eating with Ben Le-Van, unsuccessfully getting the dirt on what he actually gets up to in Cairns. Young, pretty girls come up to our table every 10 minutes to talk to him, flirt with him and ask for work. Two Chilean girls who look like models plead with him for more waitressing shifts at one of his restaurants. Two German girls ask about jobs, and when they tell him that they're trying to save money to buy a car, he mentions an old Lancer that he has parked in a paddock that they may be able to use. Ben seems to be the go-to man for everything around here.

Flash.

There on the middle of the dance floor is the Swedish girl who I saw asleep with the English guy in the bunk opposite me back in Byron Bay. There at the bar is the whingeing English girl from my day at Cape Tribulation. And there, sitting at a table in the beer garden are Mark, Ed, Brad and Chris, the four English guys with guitars, who I met on Fraser Island. They're talking to Vashti, Emma and Mel, the three English girls I met on the boat in the Whitsundays. I introduced them an hour earlier.

* * *

Flash.

Sabrina and Martina show up, and 5 minutes later so does my old lake-swimming partner Jeff. The girls are heading to the Reef and Cape Tribulation over the next two days, and then travelling inland to Alice Springs. Jeff is going back to King Island for a couple of weeks' work on the farm, then taking a trip from Adelaide up to Ayers Rock before returning home.

Ben buys everyone drinks and the Swiss girls ask me to taste theirs, as they've ordered mixed spirits.

'These are very strong,' says Sabrina. 'I think they are doubles.'

'I think our new friend is trying to make us drunk,' says Martina.

Flash.

'I make an effort to steer clear of the Brits,' someone tells me.

What makes this comment strange is it actually comes from a Brit. Mike tells me he's 27, although I notice that Martina, who he's linked up with over the past couple of days, thinks he's 23. I was feeling strangely protective towards the Swiss girls, so I was wary of Mike, but he turns out to be smarter, friendlier and more perceptive than I'd imagined.

'When you're hanging out with other English people,' he tells me. 'You can feel yourself just drinking and partying all the time, and not seeing things or meeting other people.'

This guy was giving Brit backpackers a good name. Mike was initially a bit worried coming all the way to Australia and travelling by himself. He coyly admits that he took the Oz Experience up the east coast, a hop-on-hop-off bus that's the equivalent of a Contiki tour. He confesses to feeling a bit embarrassed that Sabrina and Martina, eight years younger than him, are doing it themselves on Greyhound buses.

Mike's travels have taught him something about himself, and something about the nature of travelling itself. For instance, he stayed with a friend's family in Perth when he first came to the country, and speaks fondly of the time he spent there.

'From staying with them, I got an idea of the overwhelming friendliness of Australians,' he says. 'They'll do anything for you. My friend had to work for the first two weeks I was there, but her friends knew I was home by myself so they'd phone and invite me out places. They didn't know me, but they wanted to look out for me.

'My friend's mother even said, 'Mike, I want you to think of me as your Perth mother while you're here."

By contrast, his trip up the east coast, riding the tour bus and staying in backpackers hostels, hadn't brought him into contact with the real Australia. I was only the fourth Australian he'd gotten to know in the last four weeks. As for Gilligan's, the hostel and attached bar where we were currently drinking, he was less than flattering.

'I wouldn't stay in this place,' he said. 'I'm against this hotel-isation of hostels. The pool, the flashy bar, the flatscreen TVs, the corporate water feature outside.

'A backpackers should have a dirty, murky little pool, basic rooms, and space with tables and a barbecue. No airconditioning, no TV, bedbugs optional. That's what travelling is about.'

Flash.

I'm sitting with Vashti in the beer garden when a skinny, tall Australian guy sits down at our table and introduces himself as Evan. He talks almost exclusively to Vashti so I presume he's going to try to chat her up. As he starts talking, she grabs my hand under the table and keeps holding onto it.

Evan spoke in short sentences with gaps between them and fixed Vashti with his eyes, which never appeared to blink. Occasionally he'd look across at me for a second, possibly checking to see if I'd disappeared yet.

But if Evan is trying to chat her up, he's going about it in a very strange way. He starts telling us about a woman he met in Sao Paolo when he was travelling in Brazil. This woman affected him deeply and profoundly. In fact, he seems incapable of talking about anything apart from 'the queen of the slums'. Yes, that's what he called her.

'They called her the queen of the slums.' Pause. 'She was beautiful.' Pause. 'The most beautiful woman I have ever seen.' Pause. 'And she was special.' Pause. 'She had a light on her.' Pause. 'She walked like a cat.' Pause.

At this point, after the cat comment, Vashti squeezed my

hand hard, and I could feel that she was shaking, trying to stop herself from laughing out loud at Evan's story.

'We were engaged.' Pause. 'But I had to call it off.' Pause. 'I loved her.' Pause. 'But there were complications.' Pause. 'She was special.' Pause. 'There was a light on her.' Pause 'She walked like a cat.'

It seemed that Evan had one topic of conversation, and a limited vocabulary at his disposal. I checked to see if he had a drawstring emerging from his body that was being pulled so he could repeat these phrases.

After he'd mentioned that 'she walked like a cat' for the third time, I said to Vashti, 'Don't you have to get to that thing now?'

'What thing?' she asked.

'You know, the thing you told me you had to get to.'

'Oh, yeah! I forgot about that thing. Will you walk me out? Great to meet you Evan.'

And then we escaped the never-ending story of the queen of the slums who had a light on her and walked like a cat.

Flash.

'Jesus Christ!' yells the MC at PJ O'Briens. 'There is a God!'

The reason for his religious outburst is not because he has seen the light and decided to take on a life of sobriety, chastity and good works. Instead he is watching a Swedish girl take off her top and undulate on the bar to Salt-N-Pepa's 'Push It'. She's wearing a bra and a short denim skirt, and she's competing against three other girls who are in varying states of inebriation and undress.

'Are you seeing what I'm seeing here, people?' yells the MC. 'Because if you are, make some noise!'

It's Coyote Ugly night, a weekly ritual in many backpacker bars up and down the east coast. Girls in cowboy hats, bustier tops and very tight, very thin, very short shorts can often be seen wandering around hostels handing out flyers. They're trying to get punters to come and watch them writhe and shimmy like wannabe members of The Pussycat Dolls.

Between performances the MC asks for volunteers from the crowd to come up and strut their stuff for prizes, which usually include free alcohol. In the name of sexual equality, there's a competition for females and another for males. But they seem to get the male part of the show out of the way as quickly as possible, and don't seem nearly as desperate to encourage them to get their clothes off. Three out of the four blokes get down to their undies tonight anyway.

Flash.

Chris puts his mouth up to my ear.

'Baz!' he yells. He smells of alcohol, sweat and cigarettes. 'Take this.'

He hands me a fifty-dollar note.

'Can you get me a double vodka and Red Bull? And get anything you want for yourself, man. I'm going outside for a smoke.'

It's two o'clock in the morning. Chris is very drunk. I'm unsure he'll be able to get back in. He weaves his way across the dance floor in the vague direction of the door.

I buy the drinks, and come back to the booth where Martina, Sabrina and Jeff are taking a break from dancing. It's half an hour before Chris finally makes his way back to rejoin us.

'Hey, Baz! How ya doin' man?'

I hand him his drink and put the change from the fifty into his hand.

'What's this?' he asks.

'Your drink,' I say. 'And your change.'

'Whadda ya mean?'

'You gave me a fifty and said you wanted a double vodka and Red Bull, and to get something for myself too.'

'I did?'

'You did. About half an hour ago. Don't you remember?'

He looks at me with unfocused eyes and frowns.

'I can't remember a thing. Once I got outside I couldn't even remember where I was. Was I gone for a while?'

'You were. I thought you may have been barred from getting back in.'

'I don't even remember giving you the money. You could've got away with keeping it, man. You're a very honest man, Baz. You're a great guy. An excellent guy. Do you mind if I ask you a personal question?'

'Um, okay.'

'Are you gay?'

'Um, no. Why?'

'Well, I'm bi, and, you know…'

There's a gap in the conversation that isn't so much awkward as bewildering. I have just been chatted up. I think I have, anyway. I know I said that I would say yes on this trip, but should I suddenly decide to experiment with my sexuality?

Sadly—or perhaps fortunately—for you, dear reader, the answer is no.

'Why did you think I might've been gay?' I ask Chris.

'Well, you're a really good dancer, man.'

I couldn't argue with him there, although what this had to do with my sexuality I'm not sure.

And then, no lie, 'I Don't Feel Like Dancing' came on.

So, naturally, we danced.

Flash.

Closing time. The hot, drunken masses are pouring out of The Woolshed onto the footpath, the steam rising off bodies as they hit the night air. The rain is pelting down so hard that it sounds like the rhythm track to a techno record.

Everyone is going their separate ways. Chris says goodbye and heads off to catch up with his English buddies. Vashti warns me to be on the lookout for women who walk like cats. Jeff promises to call when he passes through Sydney in a month's time. The Swiss girls say they're going to harass me when they come through a couple of weeks later.

There are hugs. There are kisses. There is back-slapping. There are promises to keep in touch.

'Baz!' slurs Ben Le-Van, after he emerges from The Woolshed. 'Quick! Find out where those girls are going!'

I look over to where he's pointing and there's a bunch of four girls I've never seen before in my life.

'Let's get this after-party happening!' he mumbles to anyone who happens to be listening, which at this point appears to be no one, including me.

I'm done. Game over. The ant trail stops here.

The Go-Betweens were from Brisbane and they formed in the late 1970s, so it was remarkable they were any good at all. The fact that they articulated so much of our lives—well, the lives of Australians who were teenagers or in their twenties and obsessed with alternative music in the 1980s anyway— was a bonus.

One of the songwriters in the Go-Betweens, Grant McLennan, grew up around Cairns and on a Queensland farm, and he wrote what is now considered an Australian classic called 'Cattle And Cane', which is a reminiscence of his boyhood. He also wrote 'Bye Bye Pride', which mentions the mangroves, the dangerous water currents, and the lights down on Shields Street, the street where I'm unsteadily standing right now.

They did another great song called 'Spring Rain', and it talks about rain coming down like sheets and coming down like love. It also has a line about driving your first car with your elbow in the breeze. I love that line. It was the other songwriter in the group, Robert Forster, who wrote 'Spring Rain', and I think it was meant to be about Brisbane, but right now, in the middle of Cairns, with the rain coming down like sheets, I couldn't get these songs out of my head.

It was comforting, like unexpectedly meeting up with a couple of old friends in an unfamiliar place when you really needed to talk to someone. And yes, I'm aware that I hadn't swum the English Channel in the middle of winter, or crossed the Sahara on foot, or done a tour of duty in Iraq. But I was exhausted and my nerves were frazzled. I didn't know if I had a story here or not. I felt like an outsider who had been trying to get on the inside for a month, pressing my nose up against the glass and searching for the trapdoors that would let me slide down into backpacker world. But now here I was about to stumble back to another hostel, after another three a.m. closing.

I steeled myself under the awning of the nightclub and then hurled myself into the rain. It actually hurt my skin as it battered against me in giant drops. After about 10 seconds I realised it was futile to run. I was already saturated. So I slowed to a brisk walk. And eventually it wasn't even brisk. I ambled, and then stopped, stretched my arms out and lifted my face to the sky, letting the rain drench me to the skin.

A guy in his fifties walked hurriedly past me, throwing me a look, which started out as curiosity and then seemed to pass onto something like pity. I guess he was a local, and he was thinking that here was just another drunk, bedraggled, good-for-nothing tourist who got trashed at The Woolshed or PJ's and now couldn't even find his way home.

He didn't say anything, but I imagine just two words crossed his mind at exactly that point: 'Fuckin' backpacker'.

And right then it dawned on me.

I was a little drunk. I'd had a valuable conversation with one guy about the nature of backpacking, a useless conversation with another guy about the dark side of Cairns, and a totally weird, one-sided conversation with a guy who was obsessed with a woman who walked like a cat. I'd watched a Coyote Ugly night. I'd danced my legs down to stumps with 19-year-old Swiss girls, while screaming along to Bon Jovi's 'Living On A Prayer'. I'd been propositioned by an English guy who had the short-term memory of a goldfish.

And here's the thing—it was pretty much a normal night.

I don't know exactly when it happened. I started out trying to find out what it was to be a backpacker, what made them tick, and what they got up to. And I felt a little horrified, a little amused, and a little smug observing the worst aspects of their lifestyle.

Now I had to admit it. I'd become a backpacker by osmosis. Sometimes you've just got to go out there, immerse yourself, and let your surroundings soak you to the skin. Before you know it, you take on the characteristics of what it is you've set out to study.

'Things change over long distance,' the ghost of Grant McLennan sang in my head.

He was a wise man.

I walked through the rain, past the lights down on Shields Street, back to the hostel.

Fifteen minutes later I was in bed.

A half hour after that, four people were having sex in my room.

And I believe that's where you came in, and where I will now leave you.

Acknowledgements

Thanks and a two-for-one drinks special to:

Twit, SOC, M-L, and Klein for providing friendship, advice, love, encouragement, distractions, and/or sanity maintenance (take your pick or choose a combo) during the research and writing of this book; McNeil for Byron diversions and Drysdale for Bondi diversions; Mueller for saying 'It'd be a killer book, unless you went mad researching it—in fact, especially if you went mad researching it'; Kirsten Galliott and Alison Boleyn for commissioning the original Bondi story for *Sunday Life;* Jody Lee at ABC Books and editor Kim Swivel for making it better and getting it out there; every backpacker who shared a dorm room, a barstool, a bus seat, a beach, or a dance floor with me on the ant trail from Bondi to Cairns.